Y0-DFW-571

WITHDRAWN FROM
CANISIUS COLLEGE LIBRARY

Another Bridge

Another Bridge

Brigitte Barrell

with

Brent Filson

THE FAR HILLS COMPANY

Buffalo, New York

1992

P
811.5
.B24
1992

Copyright © 1992 by Brigitte Barrell. All rights reserved.

No part of this book may be used or reproduced in any manner without written permission from The Far Hills Company except in the case of reprints in the context of reviews. Address written requests for permission to The Far Hills Company, P.O. Box 97, Ellicott Station, Buffalo, NY 14205-0097.

Printed in the United States of America

First Edition

Library of Congress Cataloguing-in-Publication Number 91-077754

ISBN 0-9631422-7-5

Book designed and typeset by
Pageworks
4 Gibbons Circle
Old Saybrook, CT 06475

Published by
The Far Hills Company
P.O. Box 97, Ellicott Station
Buffalo, NY 14205-0097

Dedication

THIS IS MY STORY, but it does not belong to me. It belongs to all the women and children who suffer wars.

Throughout history, until very recent times, the decision to go to war has been made exclusively by men. They put on uniforms with shiny buttons and, filled with patriotism, they march off to fight for glory, the fatherland, medals, and rank. But for the women and children caught in war there is no glory, there are no medals, only suffering, death, and—for a few—survival.

May men stop making the decision to go to war, for theirs alone is not the price to pay.

Acknowledgments

THANKS TO Mary Ellen Albano, Kathleen Welch, and my secretary, Mary Tornabene, for all their help with the manuscript.

Special thanks to Louann Werksma of Wordwerks, our copy editor, for her excellent work, her direction, and her depth of knowledge.

Thank you to my dear brother, Commander Steffan, for his encouragement.

To my loving husband, for his unending patience with my preoccupation, thanks Nat.

Finally, I would like to express special gratitude to my beloved daughter, Brigitte, who is known to us as Gitti. Without her help and dedication, there would be no book.

Author's Note

THIS BOOK IS NOT A DOCUMENTARY, but the story is true. Names of most people and some places were changed to guard the privacy of the living.

Contents

1	Buffalo, New York, November 1989	1
2	Dresden, 13 February 1945	7
3	After the Storm	17
4	The Wounded Arrive	21
5	The Little People	27
6	My First Wrong Decision	33
7	Betrayal	45
8	My Search Begins	53
9	A Little Bit of Kindness	65
10	A Brush with Madness and Death	71
11	Angels in a Shed	81
12	My Mother	85
13	On to Leipzig	89
14	Chasing Another Lead	97
15	"No, My Son Is Not Here."	103
16	November 1989	107

1

Buffalo, New York, November 1989

MARGARET IS WAITING FOR ME, my Margaret; though, at first, I don't see her.

When I walk into the German Consulate, I see instead more than a dozen people waiting in the reception room. The receptionist catches my eye and shrugs and raises her eyebrows as if to say, "I have no idea where they all came from."

Walking toward my office, knowing that I have a full day's work ahead of me, I sense them staring at me. They sit on the well upholstered furniture, grim, angry, frightened, tearful. Many of them are over sixty years old, waiting to have passports renewed, pensions revalidated, legal papers notarized. Although we try to make their visit go as smoothly as possible, our efforts can only minimize, not eliminate, their anxieties. Most of the elderly in the reception room came to the United States during or shortly after World War II, and the apprehensions they show in having to be in a government office are, for me, windows upon suffering they experienced in a faraway country decades ago. Suddenly, for the first time in years, old terrors begin to stir in me. Then I see Margaret.

She sits at the end of the reception room, her old hands lying patiently on her lap, staring straight ahead with that alert, prideful, wise expression that I had known so well. I step toward her. "Margaret . . .." The word is almost in my mouth. But I don't speak. It's not Margaret sitting there. Of course, it's not Margaret. It's an old woman, a woman who looks as if she has the same pride, strength, and sweetness of Margaret. But she is not Margaret—not my Margaret. My Margaret came into my life more than a half century ago in a world that has long since disappeared. She was an old woman then. She would not be alive today. Still, in this moment of surprise and recognition, when I feel certain that the old woman's face is the face of Margaret, I am suddenly not in the West German Consulate in Buffalo, New York, in November 1989 but in a German village in the spring of 1945, standing in a cold drizzle with artillery rumbling in the distance, dressed in filthy, baggy pants, a khaki shirt, and a beret that distorts the features of my face.

A woman is handing me bread through a window, a woman who also looks like Margaret; and I am tearing off a piece and putting it into my mouth, my insides aching with hunger. I force the memory out of my mind, force myself to think of the present. I am here in the Consulate. There is the receptionist. There are the people, waiting. The sun is shining through the windows. Here is an old woman sitting in front of me. She is looking at me, curiously yet apprehensively. I approach her as if to speak, but then back away. "I'm

Buffalo, New York, November 1989

sorry," I say to her. "I thought you were somebody else." She smiles and nods once, and I walk into the anteroom of my offices.

My secretary looks at me and says cheerfully, "Good morning, Dr. Barrell."

"Good morning," I say, my voice coming out thinly around the tightness in my throat.

My secretary is a middle-aged woman I have known for years. But, coming out of my reverie, I seem to see her for the first time. She seems so young, so fresh, so healthy—just as that American officer in his freshly washed uniform seemed to me on that spring morning forty-five years ago. I stood with him beside the bridge that crossed a river to a Russian guard house, and asked him a question that led to the most fateful moment of my life.

My secretary takes my coat and hangs it up, saying, "What great news events! Is the Berlin Wall really coming down? Two newspapers and a television station have called. They want to interview you. They'll be calling back."

"Let's first take care of the people in the waiting room," I answer. "If either newspaper calls, let them know that I'll call back as soon as possible. If people from the station call, ask them if they'd like to do a live interview here in the office later in the afternoon."

I go into my office and sit down and skim through my mail, but rising in my mind is a vision from the past of the shrunken, dehydrated dead lying in the streets of Dresden. I come upon them as I ride my bicycle into that burning hell. I think at first that they are children, dead children in the streets; but coming closer, I see that they aren't children at all. They are grown-ups transformed into childlike mummies by the heat of the firestorm. My three-year-old son, who is riding on the back of the bicycle, asks, "Who are these people, Mommy?"

"Don't look, darling," I tell him. "Close your eyes."

I try to block those memories. I try to think of pleasant memories, memories of Margaret, Margaret and I spending that wonderful summer of my youth in 1930, telling stories to each other in the sunny Dresden-Blasewitz Park. But try as I might to fix my mind on Margaret and the grass and the park, all that I can think of is cold dew soaking my clothes in a forest, at night, in the closing days of the war in 1945. There is a logging road close by, and a squad of Russian troops is walking along the road. The soldier in front has a lantern, and its light swings back and forth across the muddy boots of the troops. Then the light and the soldiers move up the road and disappear into the darkness. The terror I feel from Russians being again so close to me is replaced by the pain of the soaking wet cold. I lie there trembling, my teeth chattering, unable to sleep, and so finally I get to my feet and begin walking. I walk first on the road, in the opposite direction than the Russians have taken. Then I lose my bearings and move off the road and begin stumbling through the forest. My mind is groggy from lack of sleep. But it is too cold to sleep. I must walk to stay warm. I must walk to keep searching.

Somebody knocks on my door. I look up from my mail and force my mind again to focus on the present. I am not in Germany. I am not in the war. I am here in my sunny office reading mail, getting ready to go to work.

The door opens, and a tall man wearing a suit and tie comes in. He is grinning. He is happy. Everyone I

Buffalo, New York, November 1989

meet seems happy today—except, of course, the people in the reception room. But perhaps they, too, will be happy. Maybe there's time and opportunity now for them to find an extra measure of happiness.

The man says, "Good morning. Have you done any interviews yet?"

"Not yet. I'm not quite sure what to say. It's the people over there in Germany, on the Wall, who know what's really happening."

I watch his face. There is nothing forced about his happiness today. So often he has to force himself to be light-hearted. I'm glad to see him this way. I had been wondering how he would react to the news of reunification.

He grins. "You can provide a local angle to the story."

"Maybe. We'll see."

"Anything wrong?" he asks. "You seem a little distracted."

"Am I?"

"A little." He studies me for a moment and then says, "I came by to invite you to lunch. We'll spend a little time together, alone, before you become a media star." He checks his watch. "It's nine o'clock now. I'll stop by around noon. That okay?"

"Sure. It's a date."

As soon as he is gone, I wonder what I can really say to the press. Last night, my daughter and I sat in front of our television and watched people celebrating on top of the Berlin Wall, and we cried for joy. But aside from expressing my joy, what can I really say about events that are happening in Europe? It's the German people who should speak now, not I. For more than three decades, I have made my life in the United States. I am married to an American. My children are here. My home is here. Yes, I am a German Consul, but I've been a naturalized U.S. citizen for thirty years. My life in Germany before and during the war, and during those months of searching and surviving at the end of the war, are all part of another person, a person who, in surviving, became lost. If that person could speak now, what would she say about today's images of celebration on the Wall? What would she say to the media?

The sight of the old people in the reception room, my imagining I had seen Margaret, and the images of people celebrating atop the Berlin Wall . . . maybe it's all merging into a new understanding for me. And that new understanding is that the other me, the lost Brigitte—should speak. Maybe after all these years, I must tell her story—if only to be free of it, finally.

"Time to get to work?" my secretary asks.

"Time to get to work," I answer.

2

Dresden, 13 February 1945

IT BEGAN WITH A GENTLE FLICKERING OF LIGHT around the edges of the blackout paper covering the window. It was an odd sight. I had never before seen light seeping around the blackout paper. But I was looking at that light without really seeing it, because my thoughts instead were of Dieter. I sat that night at a desk in our study writing to him.

                          Dresden

                          13 February 1945

My darling,

Another quiet evening and another letter. How many letters have I written since you went away? 100? 200? I don't know any more. And still only four answers from you in all these years. But just writing to you, being able to talk to you as if you were here, makes me feel better. The war will soon be over and we'll be together again. I know in my heart that you are safe and that somehow my letters will find their way to you, wherever you are. I love you. I miss you and find it hard to remember the last time we held each other.

I laid my pen down and looked over my shoulder. My three-year-old son, Alex, lay on a couch on the other side of the room, asleep, his head on Alexandra's lap. Alexandra, my mother, was reading. A few, very precious logs burned in a fireplace. Above the fireplace hung an original Rembrandt sketch, "The Solitaire Player," a gift from Dieter. Light from the fire flickered on the many photos of the family: weddings, children and ancestors covering the walls.

I had gathered these things together several months earlier when I had moved back home to Dresden from our bombed-out apartment in Berlin, hoping to wait out the end of the war. The apartment had been bombed while I was away visiting my husband's family in the Bavarian Alps. While there, I received a telegram from a neighbor informing me of what had happened. When I returned to Berlin and the apartment, I found doors and windows blasted off their hinges, and a cold wind blowing through the wreckage of our living room.

Coming to Dresden was a logical choice for me. Except for two brief raids against nearby rail yards, Dresden had never been bombed. The city had no industrial targets and was far away from the English airfields. Furthermore, it was a center of art, music, education, and theater, and was adorned with centuries of Romanesque, Gothic, Renaissance, Baroque, and Rococo architecture. It was commonly believed that the Allies had secretly agreed to spare Dresden, along with Kyoto, Japan. Just the day before, planes had dropped thousands of flyers on the city. My mother, Alex, and I were in the city at the time. Along with crowds of women, children, and old men, we grabbed gleefully at the flyers floating down and read with relief their declaration that the safety of the city was guaranteed.

The war *was* lost. It was only a matter of weeks before the Allies would come to the city. I knew that. I had known it for a long time. In a way, I looked forward to it. Even though Germany had lost, the important thing now was that the war would be over and that my family and I would be reunited and able to get back to living a somewhat normal life. I dreamed of those days to come, of my family's factory in Dresden providing a job for Dieter, since I was convinced that Germany's armed forces would be abolished. So, for all these reasons, I had come back to Dresden. But above all, I had come back because Dresden was home.

A loud pop in the logs startled Alexandra. She looked down and checked her little grandson and saw that he slept peacefully on. I turned back to my letter.

> Anyway, on to Alex! Alex is as happy and loving as always. He never needs to be entertained. He's always finding things to do by himself and is so sweet because he is always asking me if he can help me with my work around the house.

Out of the corner of my eye, I again saw the light at the edges of the blackout paper. I wondered if the air warden was signaling into our window with her flashlight. Even though Dresden was not expected to be bombed, blackout laws were strict. I stood up.

My mother looked up from her book. "What is it, Brix, something wrong?"

"I don't think so. I think the air raid warden was

shining her flashlight in our window. Maybe she's trying to tell us that they're not completely blacked out. I'm going downstairs to check."

I got a flashlight out of the desk drawer, switched it on, left the study, and closed the door so that light wouldn't peek out. I went downstairs and opened the front door. The sudden burst of light was like a blinding vision, like the realization of some terrible wisdom. Although it was ten o'clock at night, it was as bright as broad daylight outside. The sky was a sheet of light. I could clearly see the cobblestone street in front of our house, my neighbors' stone houses down the street, even the park off to the right where Alex and I often went. Far up on the hill above the city, our street was empty and silent. But the sky was lit up like a million little suns, like a vision of heaven opening. Then the silence was broken by the drone of far-off bombers. "God help us," I said.

I hurried back up the stairs and flung open the study door.

"What is it?" Alexandra said. "What's going on?" She must have seen the fear in my face, because suddenly she, too, looked afraid.

The sound of approaching bombers spoke for me; I didn't have to answer. She went to the window and tore the blackout paper away. Light poured in upon the delicate features of her face. Looking angry and determined, she said: "Those are pre-bombing flares lighting up targets for the bombers. Quickly. Get down to the basement."

We both reached for Alex at the same time. I got to him first and picked him up in my arms. Mother shoved us toward the door and said, "I'll get some things. You two get downstairs."

Dresden, 13 February 1945

Going out the door, I brushed against my wedding picture on the piano. It fell on the hardwood floor beside an Oriental rug and shattered, just as the hellish blaring of the sirens began. Alexandra grabbed the always-ready, small hand luggage that contained important papers, bank books, and money.

We went to the basement and sat there as we had done in so many basements on so many occasions during the war: basements in Berlin, the basement in Chemnitz where my grandmother lived, basements in Ludwigsburg while visiting friends or in-laws. Ours had become a life filled with air raids and basements—although sometimes, when you were caught outside with only doorways to crouch in, you longed for the refuge of a basement.

Constantly seeking shelter, always being rousted from sleep by air raid sirens, was a way of life during the last few years of the war. One time in Berlin, wakened by sirens, I went to the bathroom to brush my hair before going downstairs. Standing at the wash basin, I heard a loud pop behind me. A piece of shrapnel had come through the window; and if I hadn't leaned over to splash water on my face, it would have struck my head. Instead, the shrapnel hit the plaster wall and ricocheted onto the floor. Realizing that this small piece of metal had almost killed me, I had to look at it. It was stupid, and I burned my fingers picking it up, but I just had to have a look at it.

As Alexandra, Alex, and I huddled in a pool of dim electric light, the bombers, hundreds of them (some 1,800 bombers struck Dresden that night), began zooming directly over our house. This was different. In the Berlin basements, you usually could not hear the high-flying bombers. But tonight, since there were few anti-aircraft batteries in and around Dresden, the bombers came in low, with a maddening roar, skimming just over the rooftops. Bombs began exploding in the city, the concussions making the stone foundations vibrate. I felt the vibrations and the change of air pressure deep in my bones.

Alex gazed up at me, his chubby face looking for reassurance in my eyes, and asked, "Is that thunder, Mommy?"

"No, darling, those are airplanes. But you don't have to be afraid."

"Daddy wouldn't be afraid if he were here, would he?" Alex asked.

"No, he wouldn't, sweetheart."

"So *we* won't be afraid either, Mommy," he said firmly. He turned to my mother and said, "We won't be afraid, will we, Ohmi?"

It was his name for my mother. They shared a very special love for each other.

My mother, sitting beside us, her face set and her lips compressed, gave Alex a brave, almost tearful smile. Her other two grandchildren and her daughter-in-law, Christa, were in the inner city underneath the falling bombs. "No, Alex," she said, "We won't be afraid."

The bombing went on for an hour or more. You never get used to waiting out an air raid. And each wait is different in its own way. Yet it is the same in that you always pray. We prayed that night. We prayed for Christa and her two children in the city. We prayed for the people of Dresden. We prayed for the lives of everyone. Clinging to Alex, hugging one another, gazing into each other's eyes, sharing our fears and our courage, my mother and I knew that this bombing was more

Dresden, 13 February 1945

intense, more widespread, than any we had been through.

"You see what *he's* gotten us into?" my mother said. She meant Adolf Hitler: the "Madman," the "Beast," as she called him. She had always been against Hitler, even when he first came to power and seemed to be the savior of Germany. "He'll bring us only misery," she said over and over through the years. She spoke against him to many people, even strangers, when it was very dangerous to do so, when people who criticized him disappeared. Even now, even after the most recently failed assassination attempt of the past summer (How many had there already been?), and the Gestapo's rampant terror, she spoke against him, to acquaintances and strangers alike.

She was a proud, tender, often stubborn woman in her late forties who came from an old, distinguished family that had for centuries owned tracts of land and held government seats. Her forebears had hidden the Gutenberg Bible during the Thirty Years' War. She was reserved, rarely showing emotion. Yet when we children were in trouble with my father or school authorities, it was to my mother we went for love and support. She was widowed twice by war: Her first husband was killed in World War I; her second, my father, was killed on the Russian front.

The way my mother spoke so forthrightly and publicly against the Führer had always frightened me. During my teenage years, I had disagreed with her, thinking that he was a good leader for Germany. Back then, I was sheltered from the world by our family's wealth, by being a student of finishing schools, and by having a father who refused to allow politics to be discussed in the home. But after my marriage, as the cheering turned to the drone of bombers, and the posted slogans turned to casualty lists, I came to realize what my mother knew all along: He was cursed, and he had cursed our nation. Still, I could not bring myself to be so outspoken as my mother, to have her courage or even a small measure of her wisdom, wisdom born in the losses of two wars. Yet, no matter how wise she was, she could not have foreseen the events of the next few months, events that would force me to find courage and wisdom for us both.

After the bombing was over and the sirens sounded "all clear," I said, "I'll take Alex upstairs and put him to bed."

"No, we should stay down here. They might come again." In the flickering electric light, I could see deep lines at the corners of my mother's mouth. She seemed to have aged years during the bombing.

"Let me look."

I went upstairs and opened the door. Now a different light was spread across the sky, the grotesque glow of a city burning. Shadows moved like dancing demons in the street. Yet none of the houses in our neighborhood had been hit, nor even touched. My heart went out to my sister-in-law, her two children, and the more than one million souls in my dear city below. (Before the war, the city's population was some 800,000 people, but the population had swelled to 1.2 million with the influx of hundreds of thousands of refugees retreating from the eastern front.) I could do nothing right then for the people down there. My first concerns had to be with my son and my mother, in case there was another attack, as Mother predicted. I got bedding and brought it to the basement. I laid Alex on it and covered him

Dresden, 13 February 1945

and tucked him in. I then went upstairs and packed china, a few statues, and the Rembrandt sketch into boxes and cushioned them with wadded-up newspapers. The ninety or so minutes between the attacks went quickly. When I heard the sirens again and heard the next wave of bombers coming, I knew they were there to destroy the city forever. The first attack had come so unexpectedly that the realization had not sunk in. Now I knew, hearing the fresh bomber waves approaching, that it was the end: no more culture, no more history, no more architecture, no more Dresden.

When I got downstairs, Alex peeked out from the blankets. "Are the airplanes coming again, Mommy?"

"Yes, darling."

"Are they bad?"

"Yes, they're very bad."

"Why are they doing this?"

"It's this dreadful war. Try and go to sleep." I kissed him and stroked his hair softly.

The bombing was over in a little more than an hour. When the all-clear sirens sounded again, I left my mother and Alex in the basement and walked up the stairs and into the hallway and made my way around a chandelier, smashed on the white tile floor, over fallen paintings, around pieces of broken china, righting a chair here and there. Then I opened the door and stepped outside.

3

After the Storm

My way lit by the bright glow from the sky, I went up the street to the Café Louisenhof, which overlooked the Elbe River and the city, and walked out onto the terrace. A gale force wind blew. Ashes swirled all around me. I shielded my eyes from the wind and ash and looked down into the valley below. The Elbe no longer wound through the Dresden that had existed for more than 500 years but through a city engulfed in an apocalyptic firestorm. Looking down at streets filled with fire, at buildings that had become erupting volcanoes, at a seemingly endless sheet of flames stretching across the entire city, I felt my heart break, and I burst into tears.

It was strange walking back to the house. I was walking down my familiar street, going past the wrought iron fence, under the old shade trees, as I had done so many times. But now as I walked, I knew that scores of thousands of people were at this moment dying in the city below, and I felt numb and helpless. I reached the house and walked inside.

In the basement, my mother stood beside Alex, who still slept. She watched me. There was no emotion in her face. I wasn't bringing her news. She knew what had happened. But I said anyway, "It's gone. The city's gone. There's nothing left. They finished the job, and now there is no reason for them to come back. We can go upstairs."

She nodded. Her feelings, too, were put aside, on hold until she could confront them. I crouched down and slid my arms under Alex. Opening his eyes, he looked confused and frightened until he realized it was I, then he closed his eyes again and snuggled against me. He was so beautiful, so innocent, so precious. I took him upstairs, put him to bed, tucked him in, and kissed his little forehead.

Mother was walking out the door when I came back downstairs.

"Where are you going?" I asked.

"I want to see for myself."

"Go up to the Café and out on the terrace. You can see everything from there."

She nodded. She was gone for only a short time. She came back, then closed the door and walked down the hall toward me. I had turned on the hall light. We still had electricity, though the lights were flickering. Her head was lowered, and I could not see her face. She did not look at me. She went past me and into her room. A short while later, she came out carrying a canvas travel bag. Her raincoat was rolled up and strapped to the bag. She had on hiking clothes, heavy shoes, and a rain hat. "I'm going to my mother's," she said.

"Mother, please . . . . Let's wait. Let's think. Let's plan."

She shook her head. "They probably bombed Chemnitz too. Mother might need me."

"But it's more than sixty kilometers!"

She ignored that. "You have your responsibilities. And I have mine. You have to go into Dresden. You have to find out if Christa and the children survived. You made a promise to your brother that you would take care of them while he was away at war. I couldn't carry on if I knew that you weren't keeping that promise."

I nodded. I could not argue that fact with her. I knew that she had probably made this decision when we were waiting out the bombings in the basement. She had that tight-lipped look I knew so well. She had thoroughly analyzed the situation, made her decision, and would not change her mind.

"If you must leave, you have to take some food and money," I said.

"I have everything I need."

She took a deep breath. She said in a strained voice, "Goodbye, Brix." I knew how difficult it was for her to say that. Her leaving might really be a final goodbye. We embraced, but when she stepped back, her face was set with that determined look I respected so. We loved and trusted each other very much, but showing our love for one another was very hard for both of us. Even though our world had been destroyed, we still were prisoners of our personalities.

"You go into Dresden," she said.

I nodded.

"Find Christa and the children."

"I'll go as soon as it is possible."

We said goodbye at the door, and I watched as she

walked up the road in the smoky, ash-filled dawn and disappeared into the crowds of burned and wounded people coming out of Dresden.

4

The Wounded Arrive

WHILE ALEX SLEPT, the wounded began arriving on our street. I opened my house to them, offering water, bread and jam, and boiled potatoes. Though all of them drank water, only a few ate. Most were not badly injured. The badly injured would arrive later that day. Those who did appear on our doorstep were dazed and in pain and unable to cope with what had happened. One old woman sat on my steps, the skin of her face burned bright red, her clothes singed. I asked her to come into the house, but she refused. She sat there—bewildered and lost—embracing herself, rocking, and humming a song I could not quite understand.

As I tended to the injured, I found myself humming, too, humming a tune I remembered from a world that no longer existed, "South of the border, down Mexico way . . . " It was a tune the band had played at my wedding. Dieter and I had been married early in the war at my childhood church in Dresden-Blasewitz. Afterwards, we danced the night away at a friend's home, crowded with friends and members of our family. It was two o'clock in the morning when Dieter and I left and walked to the hotel beside the train station. I remember I was in stocking feet, carrying my shoes in one hand, happy and exhausted, skipping beside him and humming that tune the band had played again and again throughout the night, "South of the border, down Mexico way . . . ." The significance of that song was not known to us then. Many years later, Dieter would try to escape to Mexico from a POW camp in Arizona.

The next morning, we took a train to our honeymoon resort in the Austrian Alps. It was night when we arrived at a station in the foothills of the Alps, where we were met by a driver and a horse-drawn sleigh. We climbed into the sleigh, and the driver slipped fur-lined footbags over our feet, tucked fur blankets around us, then swung himself up onto the box and cracked a long whip in the frozen night air. The sleigh lurched forward, both of us laughing as our heads snapped back. With a jangling of many bells and the sleigh's runners crunching in snow, we glided up into the Flexen Pass. We felt snug and warm and filled with our love for each other. The Austrian Alps encircled us with their moonlit peaks, and the stars shone bigger than we'd ever seen them.

The war seemed very far away that March evening on our way to that Austrian ski resort, even though Dieter had only a two-week leave before having to return to his submarine. We had met the previous summer at nearby Lake Fuschl. I was vacationing with friends, and he was taking a brief leave at the lake resort while his boat was being overhauled.

Although he was wearing his Navy uniform the first night we met, he talked not of war but of his desire for peace. "When for the most part you've been stationed at sea, it is distant from home and difficult to keep track of everything that is happening. But I know it must be bad everywhere. I love my country, my home, my people, as I am sure most people of other nations must. I envision a time in the future when the leaders of all nations will meet, discuss their differences, and once and for all prevent what we must suffer now. I know it's idealistic, probably even naïve, but it's what I hope for."

I nodded in agreement. I fell in love with this tall, handsome Navy officer while we talked and danced to the strains of a zither in the lodge by the lake. I felt confident that if other young men in the world shared Dieter's longings for peace, how could war prevail?

So, eight months later, as we rode on the sleigh into the Alps during that first night of our honeymoon, I still expected the war to end soon. I believed that Dieter and I would spend the rest of our lives together. Fortunately, we were unable to see the future. We did not know that the war would last for many more years; that our time together would be brief; that our separate war experiences would make us strangers to one another; and that, for me, almost two decades of struggle would have to pass before my life would become somewhat tranquil again in a far away country.

Just outside the mountain village of Stubben, the driver suddenly "whoaed" his horses and got down, muttering angrily under his breath. Ahead in the dark, some men were erecting a barricade of logs. Dieter's warm lips touched the tip of my icy nose. Then he extracted himself from the blankets and got out.

" I'll find out what's happening and be right back."

Dieter walked ahead and conferred with the driver and three local men who were shining flashlights on masses of snow, flung down by an avalanche, which blocked the road. There was enthusiastic cursing and angry waving of arms against the snow and the mountain above them that had so unceremoniously, and without any concern or consideration for those below, caused this inconvenience.

Amused by this display of local outrage, Dieter returned to the sleigh, laughing.

"We're stuck, darling. It seems we'll have to stay the night here."

"But where?" I asked, "There seem to be only a few houses here."

"One of those men is the postmaster. He's been kind enough to offer to put us up in a room above the post office."

The room we were given was small and bare, but to my delight, I saw that there were two giant goosedown comforters on the bed. As soon as the postmaster left, I was out of my coat and under the comforter and quilts, giggling, my breath steaming in the air. I laughed as I watched Dieter struggle to get out of the heavy fur coat the sleigh owner had lent him. Then he turned out the light and joined me under the quilts. In that little room, in moonlight, under quilts, we clung to each other, wanting so badly to love and be loved in an otherwise unloving world.

Waking the next morning, I found the edge of the quilt near my mouth frozen stiff from my breath. I woke Dieter with a sharp rap on the frozen material.

"Good morning, groom." He didn't stir, so I bent over close to his ear and said loudly, "Captain! Good morning!"

He opened his eyes, looking dazed, not at first knowing where he was. Then he laughed and held my face and kissed me.

The snow had been cleared from the road, and the driver, already aboard the sleigh, awaited us. Into a world of clear sky, sunlight, and sparkling snow, we ventured on.

After two weeks in the Alps, and an endless search for a place to live, we found a spacious apartment in Berlin and moved in. Eventually, and much sooner than we had hoped, Dieter received a new assignment. We did not know when we said goodbye that our separation would be permanent.

One day, a few weeks later, a telegram arrived at our Berlin apartment with the news that Dieter was missing at sea. I dropped to my knees and begged God to somehow keep him alive. In some way, I felt that God actually did answer me. Immediately, I knew without a doubt that he had been saved, that he was alive. But I did not know that I would never have him back again. Because, years later, when he finally returned to Germany, neither he nor I were the same people who had honeymooned in the Alps. He would be an intruder into my sole purpose—survival. Because by then I had been close to insanity, lost to him and to our past, lost to the madness that for me began in the fires of Dresden.

5

The Little People

SEVERAL HOURS AFTER some of the wounded began arriving on the street outside our house, Alex woke from his morning sleep. He screwed his little fists into sleepy eyes, his face puffy from deep sleep. I dressed him and gave him a snack of bread and jam. I went to the bicycle in the hallway, fit a cushion on the spring-operated clip of the carry rack, and tied the cushion down with bailing rope. I said, "Alex, we're going to see Tante Christa, Christian, and Bettina."

His face lit up. He got up on his tip-toes and jumped up and down. "Tante Christa! Tante Christa!"

He loved his Aunt Christa. Her daughter, Bettina, was his age. Christian was a year old. "Can I bring my ball?" he asked.

"Of course."

"Where is Ohmi?" he asked. "Is Ohmi going with us?"

"Ohmi left this morning to go visit Great-grandmother."

Alex looked confused.

"Alex, Ohmi is fine. She's just going to see if Great-grandmother is all right."

"What's the matter with Great-grandmother?" he asked suspiciously.

"Nothing, Alex. Everybody is fine. Ohmi will only be gone for a few days. She'll come back. Then we'll all be together again."

He smiled and nodded. "That'll be fun!"

I wheeled the bike outside and down the steps past the old woman, who rocked and keened in a faint voice, locked the door, and went out onto the street. There was less smoke in the air than there had been at dawn. The wind had died a little. Alex gazed curiously at the woman.

"Is she all right?" he asked.

"Yes, she was hurt last night. Now she's trying to get better."

"Were many people hurt last night?"

"Yes. But they'll get better."

"Was Tante Christa hurt?"

"Let's go find her."

"And Bettina and Christian?"

"We're going to go help them."

I lifted Alex up and set him down on the cushion. "Put your ball in my pack. Hold on tight! We're going to be riding downhill!"

"Wheee!" he sang.

We went down the cobblestones beside the street car tracks. I put on a brave face for Alex; but, in truth, I was heartsick about what might have happened to Christa and her children. They lived in the center of the city in a house near the *Grosse Garten* and not very far from our family factory. Christa's husband, my brother, had run the factory until he was drafted three years earlier. I had always felt close to Christa and her children. She was my age, and we shared a love for music, athletics, and Dresden. Alex loved to play with his cousins. I had wanted to search for them soon after my mother left, but I did not want to disturb Alex's sleep. I wanted to make life for him as normal as possible, an effort that I knew would take all my strength and ingenuity.

As I bicycled into the city, I found little destruction at first. The houses I passed were intact, though as I got farther down the hill I first saw broken windows and, later, black holes where roofs had been. As we rode along, we passed old men, women, and children coming up the street out of the city. They were in worse shape than the people who first came to my house. Their faces were black. Their clothes were nearly burned off their bodies. They were weeping, staring blankly, holding their heads, staggering aimlessly. Some were refugees dressed in motley clothing found along the way on their trek west. They had escaped the advancing Russian armies and were in Dresden's streets, waiting to continue their journeys, when the bombs fell. Others, well dressed, apparently had been bombed out of their houses. All of them were exhausted.

"Who are those people?" Alex asked.

"They're people who are hurt. Don't look, darling. Keep your eyes closed."

I knew that I shouldn't have brought Alex, but I had no other choice. I couldn't have left him alone in the house. As we got closer to the river, heavily damaged houses appeared through the thickening smoke. I saw flames leaping from windows, large cracks in the masonry walls, toppled chimneys, walls smashed open,

Another Bridge

exposing views into the homes. They looked much like the houses I had seen after the bombings in other cities. My perspective was so distorted by my war experiences that, when I saw those houses on this side of the river, I actually felt my spirits lift a little. I thought that the bombing might not have been so bad, certainly no worse than I had experienced before, and that the city might have some life left yet. But as I crossed the bridge to the *Altmarkt* I saw that I was wrong. I was looking at a new and more terrible kind of devastation.

The buildings, the beautiful, historic buildings of old Dresden, were on fire and had begun crashing down. (It was only later that they collapsed and the famous photos of Dresden's flat ruinscape were taken.) Thousands of dead were strewn in the flame-blackened, rubble-littered streets and piled along the banks of the river. *Why are only children killed?* I thought, seeing only tiny people, tiny people in oversized clothes. I took a closer look, and my head started to spin. This was grotesque, unreal. I wasn't looking at children but grown-ups—the charred, dehydrated bodies of grown-ups. Little people, blackened and dry, almost like statues. They were stiff, as if they had struck a pose. I realized that the firestorm had raced through the city and caught the fleeing people in midstride. In an instant, the tremendous heat had sucked them dry and left them captured in their moment of death, their screams still etched on their dead faces.

"Mommy, why are these people lying down? Did they fall? Should we help them up?"

"No, darling. Leave them alone. They're asleep. Now don't look. Don't look anymore."

All around us were flames, smoke, and dust. Inhuman moans and screams were muffled by the roar of masonry walls crashing down. The sweet, awful, unforgettable smell of burned human flesh sickened me. We traveled through a kaleidoscope of bizarre images: A crocodile from the destroyed zoo lay dead on the steps leading to a bank; a llama followed us, making an unearthly humming noise, apparently looking for water or food.

I turned onto Christa's street and saw that her great, stone, hundred-year-old villa was a heap of smoking rubble. I lifted Alex off the bike and told him to sit down and wait for me. Then I climbed among the piles of hot stones calling out for Christa and the children. No one answered. Except for the dead lying among rubble in the street, there was no one in sight. Usually, if people survived a bombing, they scrawled a message on the pavement or stones with chalk. Frantically, I looked for the words *Wir Sind Raus, Christa*, but couldn't find writing anywhere. The stones were much too big and heavy for me to move. If Christa and her children were buried beneath them, I could do nothing to help. I prayed that somehow they had escaped.

(They *had* escaped. After the war, I learned they had gotten out between the first and second bombing.)

I put Alex back on the bike. "Let's go home." I said.

"But what about Tante Christa?"

"They're not here now. We'll come back another day."

He looked at me. "But you promised!" And then suddenly there was a kind of understanding in his face. He nodded and dropped his eyes. "All right, Mommy. We'll go home."

"Don't look anymore, darling. Don't look at anything. Promise?"

"I promise," he said and put his little hands over his eyes.

I pedaled quickly back to our house, thinking that if I could only get safely home, the worst of our experiences would be over. But I was wrong about that, as wrong as I would be about so many things in the weeks ahead.

6

My First Wrong Decision

AS DRESDEN'S ASHES COOLED, the disposal of the dead went on day and night. Endless lines of hand- and horse-drawn wagons carried piles of human dead to be buried on the outskirts of town. Dead were also carried to the *Altmarkt*, the focus of the bombing (where temperatures had risen up to 1,000 degrees Fahrenheit during the night of the firestorm). There they were stacked, doused with kerosene, then set afire with flame throwers. The smell of burning dead and the smell of the decaying dead, buried in cellars under hills of rubble, hung in the air day in and day out.

During those days, many people came to my house on the hill, overlooking the ruined city, for shelter and food. Often, I would have up to twenty people at one time. They were dazed, depressed, bewildered. Some were badly wounded and burned and constantly cried out in pain. They would stay for a day or two, gather their strength, then depart for the West, trying to stay ahead of the advancing Russians. One awful thing was on everybody's mind: *The Russians are drawing nearer.*

There was no electricity or gas at the house and, for days on end, no water. We lived on bread and jam, canned food, and potatoes that had been stored in the basement. Often, I had to bicycle thirty kilometers for bread, Alex always with me on his little seat on the back of the bike.

Alex was my constant concern. Wanting to protect him from the hell around us, I kept him close by me. I felt awkward that my mother and Dieter were not there to make decisions for Alex and me, but I looked upon my new situation of being in charge as only temporary. I did not let Alex out except to accompany me when I went for bread or to play in the garden behind our house. He was, as always, such a happy, friendly child. He did not need to be entertained. He always found ways to play by himself, spending endless hours making castles in the earth with a spoon or helping me now and then with chores around the house. He loved working with me, washing dishes, sweeping, washing clothes. "I want to help, Mommy!" was his constant refrain. If there wasn't a job to do, he would make one up. One day, I found him combing out the fringe on the Oriental rugs. He worked diligently and then clapped his hands with excitement when he decided the job was done. From time to time, he questioned me about the llama and the crocodile lying on the bank steps, the burning buildings, the dead in the streets, and the refugees coming to our house. I answered always that there had been a terrible fire in which people had died and gone to heaven, and that we were helping take care of the survivors. I told him, too, that as long as we were together he would be safe and happy.

My First Wrong Decision

"Are you going to die, Mommy?" he sometimes asked.

"No, darling, I won't die."

"Then you won't leave me like Ohmi did?"

"I told you, Ohmi will be gone for only a few days."

"I know."

"Alex, I won't leave you. I'll always be with you."

"And I won't leave you. I'll help you. And when Daddy comes home, we'll both help you around the house. We'll never leave each other. We'll always help each other. And we'll help people that need help. You and Daddy and I!"

With each passing week, living in Dresden became increasingly difficult. I decided to take Alex to a friend's home, Castle Hirschfeld, on the Elbe River. I had been there before and thought it would be a safe place for us to stay until after the war, until we could return to Dresden. I stored valuables in the basement and packed a small backpack with some clothes, jewelry, personal papers, and money.

With Alex on the back seat, I bicycled away from Dresden and soon, under a clear sky, pedaled down country roads that curved through pine woods and open fields and meadows. Oddly, the war had not yet come to this pocket of the countryside, though the constant rumbling of distant artillery fire could always be heard. The yards around the stone farmhouses were well cared for. Smoke rose from their chimneys. There were many refugees on the road, carrying packs and suitcases. Some had piled their possessions in little four-wheeled, hand-drawn wagons, on bicycles, and even on children's buggies. They were all streaming toward the West. But I was going the opposite way. I was going toward the East, toward the castle on the

Elbe east of Dresden. I did not think that I was making the wrong decision. My rationale was that these refugees from the eastern provinces of Germany had no place to stay and so were moving westward until they found shelter. But I knew that I could find shelter in the castle. So, foolishly, I did not question that Alex and I were going against the refugee tides, toward the Russian front, toward our private disaster. The sun warmed us in the chilly air; and as I pedaled, I felt the torpor that had weighed on me since the bombing weeks before begin to fall away.

Alex asked, "Do you think Tante Uli and Onkel Fritz will be at home when we get there?"

"Sure they will. Do you remember when we visited their house?"

"Yes Mommy! They live in a big house like Uncle Claus'."

"And what do they have there that you love to ride?"

"Ponies!"

"Right!"

"And they have cows who say 'Moooo', and ducks who go 'Quack', and roosters that wake you up in the morning, 'Cock-a-doodle-dooo'!"

He flapped his little arms, and nearly pitched from the bike, and we laughed happily going down that road.

We traveled many hours, now and then pausing to eat bread we bought in a store. Biking was easy. Heavy military vehicles had not yet chewed up the asphalt roads. Sometimes I pedaled, sometimes I walked the bike. I don't remember getting tired. In fact, the farther we got from Dresden, the stronger I felt. Once in a while, Alex would complain that his bottom hurt, and

My First Wrong Decision

I would stop and lift him down from the bike. We would sit by the side of the road and rest, or walk alongside the bike. Then I would lift him back on the seat, and we would ride together again along the road to Hirschfeld.

The sun was dropping behind trees on the far side of a vineyard when he said, "Are we almost there?"

"Yes, almost there."

"Are we going to stay in the castle long?"

"No, darling, just until Daddy and Onkel Pott come home. Then we'll all go back to Dresden and live there together."

"When will that be?"

"Soon, Alex. I do hope soon."

"We'll do that when the war is over?"

"The war is over. For you and me, it's over."

"Did Daddy win the war?"

"When he comes home, you can ask him yourself."

"Can we go fast on the bike again?"

"Sure! Let's go!"

The road swung back toward the Elbe, and the castle, standing on a promontory above the river, came into view. A few minutes later, we were there.

When I entered the cobblestone courtyard, I was surprised to see pieces of broken furniture scattered about. A dozen or so Polish refugees came through the entrance door, walked down the steps, and went past me. Even if they hadn't been speaking Polish, I would have known they were not German. Liberated from labor-conscript factories to the West, there were mostly middle-aged men making their way back toward Poland in groups of twenty or thirty, and a desperate hatred of Germans showed in their faces. They eyed me as I passed them. A vague impulse warned me not to enter the castle. But, having not yet learned to act upon my instincts, I did not obey that impulse.

I took Alex off the bike and lifted it up the steps and through the door. The inside had changed totally since I had last been there. The tapestries, the decorative Renaissance armor and weapons, the paintings, and the Oriental rugs were gone. Broken furniture was scattered all around. The floors were filthy with tracked-in mud; the smell of urine hung in the air. There was a constant coming and going of Polish and German refugees. Nobody spoke. Everyone seemed to be coping with their own miseries in silence. My friends were nowhere in sight. Clearly, this was no place for Alex and me to live. I leaned the bike against the wall, sat down, and drew Alex into my arms, uncertain as to what to do next.

A number of Polish men walked past, glancing at me and my bicycle. I realized that the bicycle would be a valuable possession for anyone traveling on the roads and that if a group of those men wanted to take it, I could not stop them. There were no laws, no police, nothing to stop them from doing whatever they wanted.

Alex had fallen asleep in my arms, and I was undecided whether to keep sitting there and let him sleep or rouse him and get out of the castle.

"You shouldn't be here alone." The words were German, the husky voice that of a woman. I looked up. The woman standing over me was in her twenties, dressed in men's trousers and a jacket. One hand held the hand of a four-year-old girl. Her free hand she held out to me. "My name is Greta Witt." I looked into her

My First Wrong Decision

broad, honest face and felt I had found a friend. I told her my name, and we shook hands. She had a confident, reassuring grip. She told me that she was the wife of an Army doctor and had been forced from her home in East Saxony by the threat of advancing Russians. She had spent the past two days at the castle.

"There's a room at the back. Nobody goes there. I've found a key to the room. We can keep it locked. There are two beds with mattresses. I found two sheets, and I have a blanket. Will you share the room with us?"

Greta was a welcome sight. She was strong, healthy, and resourceful. Her daughter Margot was a delight, as uncomplaining, confident, and cheerful as Greta was. She and Alex would make wonderful playmates.

Meeting Greta was a stroke of fortune. I felt that she was a person who could take charge of our lives and help us make the right decisions. Greta and I decided to remain together throughout the duration of the war.

That night we stayed in the room overlooking the river. Moonlight danced on its surface, and only the distant thunder of artillery fire gave evidence that we were in a war. The view reminded me of the view from the Gerhardt Hauptman house in Dresden where I had spent most of my childhood. We had moved there when I was eight from our house in the city, the same house that now lay in ruins. The house was in the city's outskirts in a wealthy neighborhood, its tall, arched windows opening onto terraces and porches that looked out on a meadow and the Elbe river below the meadow. On summer evenings, pleasure steamers went up and down the river; and, lying in bed, I could see their strings of Japanese lanterns and hear the orchestra music wafting on the soft, warm air. I loved the river; its beauty became an important part of my childhood. But in that castle room that first night away from Dresden, my childhood by the river seemed a half-forgotten dream.

During the night, the stone-walled room became cold. I had not brought blankets. I thought my friends would still be living in the castle. Greta had only one blanket, which we used to cover the children. The next morning, I decided to go back to Dresden, to get blankets and the remaining cans of food, then return to the castle.

"Let Alex stay with me," Greta said. "He's better off playing with Margot than spending uncomfortable hours on the bike. Without him you can travel faster and bring more things, as well."

I agreed. Alex agreed. He wanted to play with his new friend, not go on another arduous bike trip. I said goodbye to Alex, told him I would be back that day or the next, and bicycled back to Dresden.

At first, I thought I could get there by noon and return by early evening, but more refugees crowded the roads than the day before. They seemed more fearful, and those I passed in the afternoon hurried more than did the refugees I had encountered that morning. Also, the sounds of artillery fire were much closer. Here and there a German panzer clanked along the road between the crowds of refugees, the crews' faces haggard and streaked with dirt and smoke. Slowed by two flat tires, I did not arrive at my house in Dresden until late afternoon. I decided to spend the night at the house rather than risk trying to get back to the castle in the dark. At first light, I started out, a load of canned goods and blankets on the back of my bike. The distant

My First Wrong Decision

artillery fire was louder than ever. Instead of rumbling like faint thunder, it cracked sharply through the air.

After traveling for about an hour, I rounded a bend and saw a large number of refugees streaming toward me. Instead of trudging doggedly along as usual, they were in a panic. Scores of them had left the road and were stumbling across muddy fields, tripping and falling, getting up, and, splattered with mud, stumbling on. I rounded another turn, past a grove of pines, shoving and jostling against the refugees, and saw a half dozen German soldiers working frantically around an antitank gun. Wearing muddy, tattered uniforms, they resembled refugees themselves. The gun was on pneumatic tires and, positioned under the boughs of the trees behind a hummock of earth, pointed toward a highway crossroads. There were no refugees between me and the gun emplacement. As I walked toward the gun, one of the soldiers, who dug frantically with a spade, looked at me. His face under his helmet visor was hollow-cheeked. His eyes were glassy. He shouted at me to turn around and go back, but I kept walking toward him. The other soldiers, half mad with fear and exhaustion, shouted angrily at me to get away. I saw still more soldiers. They were strung along a line inside the grove of trees, digging with shovels. The soldiers at the gun were shouting at each other and shouting at me. I found myself shouting back at them.

"I've got to get down that road."

"Get back! Get out! The Russians are on the other side of the highway!"

"I've got to get back to my son!"

The soldier digging beside the gun raised himself up. "Get away! Get away! Or we'll make you go away!"

I walked into the woods. The soldiers digging in the woods screamed at me to go back up the road. I moved into the pine trees until they could not see me. Refugees had picked the ground and the lower branches of the trees clean for firewood, so I could maneuver my bike easily through the forest. I decided to circle around the soldiers' flank. I thought that if I could stay out of sight in the trees and make a wide enough circle, I could get around their line and then move cross-country, paralleling the highway before returning to it a few miles up the road.

There was a racket in the pines far above me. It sounded like birds flying through. Pine boughs and pine needles rained down. The odor of shattered green wood and pine resin filled the air. I heard the CRACK of the nearby anti-tank gun. In the distance, beyond the crossroads, there was the crash of an exploding shell. Ahead, I saw the shapes of German soldiers in the pines. They were lying on their sides, digging frantically, shouting.

Gunfire rattled from the woods on the far side of the crossroads. The Russians *had* arrived. The Germans were engaged in a holding action. I was in the middle of a battle for the crossroads. I dropped to the ground, more angry than frightened. I was furious that this stupid fighting would prevent me from getting through. I realized that if I kept trying to get through, I might get killed. *Then* what would happen to Alex?

I had no choice but to lie there, try to wait out the fighting, and move away during a lull. I waited an hour or two, pressed flat against the earth, listening to the firing, thinking of Alex waiting for me in the castle, Alex trusting that I would be back. I longed for Dieter

My First Wrong Decision

or my mother to be with me. They would know what to do.

Then my moment came. During a break in the firing, I got up and, leaving my bike behind, ran madly, flooded with fear, clawing through thickets, until the firing, which had resumed again, seemed a good distance away. But as I left the woods, I became caught up once again in the throngs of refugees. The fighting blocked the refugees' way. If I waited in the panicking crowds, I would be trapped and would have to spend the night in the open, exposed to more fighting. My only choice was to move away from them by returning to Dresden.

7

Betrayal

IT WAS LATE AFTERNOON OF THE SECOND DAY when I finally got back to my house in Dresden. Exhausted, I decided to sleep and figure out a new tactic in the morning. At dawn, I awoke to hear voices on the street outside my window, voices that made my heart stop. They were the voices of Russians.

I looked out the window. Two Russian soldiers in muddy brown uniforms stood near my front door. It was the first time I had ever seen Russian soldiers. They were talking to one of my neighbors, a woman in her fifties.

I couldn't believe my eyes. The Russians must have entered Dresden during the night. I had heard no sounds of fighting in the streets, only the distant rumble of artillery. But there they were. They had their rifles slung over their shoulders. They seemed relaxed. Apparently, they hadn't recently been engaged in combat. They must have just moved into what was left of the city without a fight. The fighting I had encountered at the crossroads had been just some kind of desperate, unsuccessful action.

My neighbor was speaking to them in German, but she was too far away for me to understand what she was saying. The soldiers listened to her, then spoke to each other.

The woman pulled the sleeve of one of the soldiers and gestured angrily toward the house. She and the soldiers walked up the path and knocked on the door.

At first I thought I wouldn't answer. But then I realized that people must have seen me come into the house the night before. The woman knew that I was here. If I didn't answer, they might break down the door and come looking for me. Wanting to appear nondescript, I drew out my husband's trousers and shirt from a closet and put them on, cinching the big waist with one of my belts. Wearing Dieter's things, I began to feel somewhat confident. Thinking that they might search my knapsack, I took my jewelry out and put it in the cuffs of the trousers. Then I went downstairs and, though not as confident as I wanted to be, opened the door.

Being close enough to touch two Russian soldiers, I felt the blood drain from my face. The woman began shouting angrily at me. I had seen her less than half a dozen times since I had returned to Dresden a few months before. She lived in a house a few doors up the street. We had never spoken to each other. Now her face was purple and twisted and fearful as she shouted at me. "Take her away! Her husband's a war hero! He's been given honors, medals!"

One soldier grabbed my pack. The other grabbed my arm and pushed me down the walk. I tried to speak, to ask, *Please, why are you doing this?* But I couldn't get the words out. My lips moved but no sound came out. I looked at the woman. She turned away, unable to look me in the eyes. She had betrayed me in order to save herself. Now that the Russians were in the city, moving into the hillside houses that had survived the firestorm, people were trying to survive any way they could—even by betraying their neighbors.

They took me to the Café Louisenhof from where I had first seen Dresden's destruction. The doors and windows were flung open, and Russian soldiers were everywhere: coming and going, sitting at tables, writing on papers, examining maps, cleaning dismantled rifles, sleeping on the floor, laughing, arguing. When I was pushed inside, many of them stopped what they were doing and looked at me. I felt my skin crawl underneath my husband's floppy clothes. I was pushed toward a door in the back of the Café. I thought: *I can't go through that door. If I do, I'll never come out again.* I clutched at the side of the door, but I was pushed through and into a hallway. *God, please, don't let this happen*, I prayed. I was shoved down a hallway and down a set of stairs to a storeroom door. One Russian pulled on the door. He said something to his companion, who went up the stairs. Alone for a few moments with the Russian, I pushed my back against a corner of the wall, wanting to melt into the stone. I could feel his eyes staring into me. Fear pressed like a heavy iron bar on my chest, crushing my breath. Then the Russian came back down the steps. He slid a key into the lock and opened the door. They shoved me inside and closed and locked the door. I heard their boots on the stones as they went back upstairs.

I was in a stone-walled, windowless storage room, lit by a flickering electric light bulb screwed into a ceiling fixture. The floor-to-ceiling racks were bare. There was a horrible odor. Two middle-aged women crouched on the floor, staring at me with dazed expressions. They both wore rumpled skirts and mud-spattered coats. Their hair was uncombed and matted with mud. I asked, "What are we doing here? Why have they brought us here? Who are you?"

They said nothing, staring at me with eyes that did not seem to see me. One of the women had a bruised eye. The other had blood caked in her nostrils. I realized what the bad odor was. The women had relieved themselves in a large tin can that stood in a corner. The air was so oppressive that I nearly vomited. After a few minutes, one of the women said, "They'll be back. They'll be back for you. They'll be back for all of us."

"What did they do to you?" I asked.

They did not answer. No one spoke again. Hours went by. Two more middle-aged women were brought to the room. They too were frightened, disheveled, and dazed. Like the others, they would not speak. After awhile, the light went off. We remained for hours in the dark. Over and over, I prayed, *Please don't let me die. Please don't let them do this to me. Don't let them come here and take me. Alex needs me. I can't die. I have to get through this. Whatever it is, I have to survive it and get back to Alex.*

After hours of waiting in the dark, the heavy cellar door swung open, and I blinked and squinted in the sudden light. A Russian soldier, wearing not a helmet but a cloth cap, peered in. I felt my insides squeeze tightly. This was it. They were coming for us. The soldier pulled his head away from the door. I heard his hobnail boots ringing on the stone steps as he walked away. He hadn't closed the door completely. A faint band of light shone through where it was ajar. I walked to the door and opened it slightly. Faint daylight, coming from the door at the top of the stairway, illuminated the cellar steps. There was no one on the steps, no one in the doorway at the head of the steps. I pushed the door open and went up two or three steps.

One of the women complained: "Get back. What are you doing? Are you crazy?"

"I'm leaving," I said.

"They'll kill us. If you try to escape, they'll kill us all."

I went up and looked through the door into the hallway. No one was there. I went quietly down the hallway and opened the back door and stepped outside.

I walked away from the Café, carefully putting one foot in front of the other, trying to look relaxed. There were a few people walking on the street, but no Russian soldiers. I turned a corner and broke into a mad run through rubble-filled streets. I ran until my lungs were ready to burst. But no one chased me. No one followed me. After resting briefly on the front steps of a bombed-out building, I began my trek back to the castle.

I had no bike, no pack, no blankets, no plan—except to get back to the castle as fast as I could. There were many refugees on the road but few Russian troops. The Russians had gone quickly through the area and had continued westward to meet the Americans. There was no fighting in this area because there were no German troops left to fight.

I walked until it got dark. Then I walked on and on through the dark. Whenever I heard somebody coming

Another Bridge

toward me, I got off the road and lay down and waited for them to pass. Many people passed me that night. I did not know who they were: Germans or Russians, soldiers or civilians—moving like spirits through a black hell.

I reached the castle early in the morning. This time, the courtyard was completely empty. I ran inside and found the lower rooms empty, too. Calling, "Alex! Alex! Greta!" I ran to the back of the castle and flung open the door of the room we had stayed in. No one was there. Greta's suitcase and clothes were gone. The only thing left behind was Alex's little digging spoon, which lay on the floor under the window. I ran in a panic through hallways calling Alex's name, then hurried out into the courtyard. I saw an old man walking across the courtyard. I hurried up to him, out of breath, and said, "Sir, sir, did Greta tell you where she was going?"

He scratched his head and looked at me with bewildered eyes. "Greta, should I know Greta?" Then I recognized him. He was the castle's gardener. A few years before, on a visit to the castle, I had seen him. Back then, he was neat and always clean-shaven. Now his clothes were filthy; pieces of food were stuck in his whiskers; and his hair fell uncombed over his ears.

"Don't you remember me?" I said. "I was here visiting the owners. You showed me your rose bushes."

He shook his head. "No, I don't know you."

"Look, I stayed here two nights ago. I was with a German woman. She had her four-year-old daughter with her. I have a three-year-old son. I left him with her. I left to get blankets and food in Dresden. But now that I've come back, I can't find her. She and the children are gone. Do you know them? Have you seen them? Do you know where they went?"

He looked at me with blank eyes.

I described Greta, her child, and Alex again. He shook his head. He pointed to the road. "I don't know them. But if they're not here, they must have gone west. Everybody is going west. You should go too. There's no one in the castle today. But soon there will be Russians."

"Have you seen Russians?"

"Some Russian soldiers came this morning. They left. But there will be others. So you'd better go now."

He began to walk off, then stumbled. I caught his arm to keep him from falling. He sat down on a stone bench, his big, work-toughened hands clutching his knees. He looked very tired and confused.

"Shouldn't you leave, too?" I asked.

"I have my gardens. I can't leave my gardens," he said.

I walked up the road toward Hirschfeld. On both sides of the road, refugees streamed out of the village and turned onto the highway that led west. I did not know which way to go. Alex and the others could have gone anywhere: into the village, or onto roads leading out of Hirschfeld to the west and north.

I needed to think, to think about what to do next. Alex was gone. It was my fault. Alex was gone. I had caused it. I was the only person he could depend on, and I had failed him. For the first time in my life, I had been left alone to make decisions; and all I could do was make one mistake after another. Somewhere Alex was alone and suffering, and I couldn't help him. I began to sob desperately.

Another Bridge

I couldn't give in to my emotions. I had to get control of myself. I had to think clearly, to make plans to find him. It was up to me to make the kind of decisions that Dieter or my mother would make. If I didn't find him, no one could.

I knew that if I went into town and began asking about Alex's whereabouts, while Greta and Alex were in fact taking the road west, I'd be losing precious time. But if I took that road, and they were in the village, I'd be putting more distance between us.

"I've got to find him or die trying," I said. "If he's alive, I'm going to find him."

8

My Search Begins

I DECIDED TO LOOK FIRST IN THE VILLAGE, asking women (only women and children were left) if anyone had left a message for me, if anyone knew where the German refugees from the castle had gone; but no one had any answers. No one had seen Alex, Greta, or Margot.

Some of the old women felt badly for my plight. Others did not care, did not want to talk to me. With so much grief in the world, many people did not want to hear of more. In addition, everybody was frightened. People were saying aloud or through the expressions of their faces, "What new horrors will tomorrow bring?" After several hours of asking questions, I headed west on the highway with the crowds of refugees.

I had nothing but the clothes on my back: my husband's trousers, khaki shirt, and an old beret that I found in the street in the village of Hirschfeld the first day of my search. I had stuffed my hair inside the beret and pulled it down across my eyebrows. It was too small and made the skin of my forehead bunch over my eyebrows, distorting my features so that, hopefully, I would be less likely to attract the attention of Russian soldiers on the lookout for young women.

The first day or two I went without food. The only thing I put in my stomach was water I drank from brooks.

At one town, I stopped in an administrative office to apply for food stamps. The clerk, a round-faced woman with short black hair and big red ears, gazed at me suspiciously from behind piles of papers on her desk.

"What do you want?" she asked.

"I was told I could get food stamps here."

"Very well. Name?"

I told her.

"Address?"

"I'm a refugee. I have no address."

"You must be living somewhere."

"On the streets. In the forest with other refugees."

"No address. No food stamps."

"I can give you the address of my house in Dresden, but it has been confiscated by the Russians."

"You must have a permanent address here. We cannot be giving food stamps to anybody who comes along. We would run out."

"But I must have some food."

She looked around me. Other people had come in and were standing in line behind me. "Next," she said.

"I'm looking for my son. I can't have a permanent address."

"No address. No food stamps. Next."

The people behind me began murmuring impatiently. I felt a hand on my shoulder. An old woman pushed me out of the way. "Get out," she said. "Move on. It's my turn."

"Leave," the clerk said. "Or I'll have you thrown out."

I went out into the street, knowing that, as far as officialdom was concerned, I did not exist. In a way, I could not exist, not in my old way, and not in any new way, not until I found Alex.

I could not go on much longer without getting something to eat. I should have taken money with me, but in my haste to dress in Dresden while the Russian soldiers were knocking on the door, I had taken only jewelry. I thought of exchanging my jewelry for food but knew that if I was to find Alex, I would have to use the jewelry to buy information and passage between the American and Russian lines.

I left the masses of refugees traveling along the main roads in the hope I would have a better chance of finding food on my own. I came upon a railroad crossing, beside which stood a small stucco house for the crossing master. I thought of him, whoever he was, with his lifetime job to control the flow of rail traffic, to lower and raise the guard rails when trains came through. He had probably believed that he would live out his life in that small house beside the tracks. But then the war came, and his life, like the lives of most other people in Europe, had been changed forever.

I sat down in a field a short distance from the crossing and watched the house, wondering what I might find there. I remembered our family cook and how she was constantly making spinach. Like almost all children, my younger brother Pott and I hated spinach. It was the unfortunate duty of our governess,

Winifred, to make sure we ate it. "Spinach is the healthiest food of all," she would tell us. One day, we were served spinach soup in the children's room, where we usually ate (our parents took their meals in another part of our house); and, instead of eating it, had presented the governess, after she had been absent from the room for only a minute, with the spectacle of spinach-soup-decorated walls. I wondered, what would I give now for a bowl of that spinach soup?

There were no signs of life around the house except for a flock of scrawny chickens in the yard. I knocked on the door. No one answered. I tried the door. It was locked. I walked around the house, looking in the windows, but it was dark inside. Nobody seemed to be there. The chickens had moved to the far end of the yard and were pecking in the mud while keeping an eye on me. I went down into a shallow ravine out of sight of the house. I took off my shirt and called to the chickens. "Here Chick. Chick. Chick." After awhile, one approached me. I leaped forward and threw my shirt over it. I grabbed it and felt the beating of a tiny heart under warm feathers. Squawking and flapping, it broke away from me and ran off. As I watched it disappear around the side of the house, I felt worse about having tried to steal a chicken than having failed in the attempt.

Days passed into weeks. One day, I walked through a cold drizzle into a village and saw a woman sitting at the window of her house, eating bread and jam. The window was right on the street, and she was no more than a meter away from me. I stood there, transfixed.

My consciousness seemed to slip to one side. I remembered Margaret and the first time we met. It was 1930, and I had found her sitting in the park in front of

My Search Begins

the grounds of our residence. It was a sunny, summer day, spangled with motes of dandelion blow floating over meadows that fell away to the nearby Elbe River. I enjoyed eating my lunch in the park on those summer days and would often sit on the same bench overlooking the river. But on that day, an old woman sat on the bench I usually occupied. Dressed in threadbare clothes, she gazed at the river. She was very thin, sweet, frail, and proud looking. I thought of going somewhere else to eat but asked if she would mind my sitting beside her.

She smiled, and the wrinkles deepened at the corners of her eyes, those friendly, intelligent, highly perceptive eyes.

"Certainly not," she said. "Please sit down. No one owns the parks—yet!"

"I'm Brigitte. What's your name?"

"I'm Margaret, Brigitte." She looked over her shoulder at the big, stone villa, surrounded by gardens and fruit trees, on the rise behind us. "Is that your house?"

"Yes, I live there with my parents, my brothers, and my pets."

"Pets? Oh, really? I love animals. What pets do you have?"

I laughed. It seemed easy to laugh in her presence. I felt that I had known her for a long time. "All sorts, really. I love animals, too. But that's the trouble. I mean that's why I've been in trouble lately."

Margaret raised her eyebrows and scrutinized me in a kindly way. Her eyes were rheumy, the beginnings of cataract growth causing the blue of her irises to wash into the whites. "Trouble, what sort of trouble could you get into, Brigitte?"

"I'll tell you about the latest!" I explained how, during recent rains when the Elbe pushed into the lower meadows, forming tiny islands where families of washed-out moles clustered, I had gathered a dozen moles in a box and deposited them in the loose, rich soil of our gardens to begin a new life in a safer place. I told her that our gardener, a meticulous man, especially when it came to "his" gardens, almost fainted dead away when he saw the tunnels my moles had dug all through his garden. He went to my father and threatened to quit. My father sent me to my room and defused the man's anger only by guaranteeing that I would stay away from the gardens.

Margaret placed her hand on my sleeve and laughed.

"Well, maybe you think it's funny, but you don't know how awful my father looks when he's angry."

Margaret laughed harder, though there was nothing derisive in that laughter, only amusement and understanding.

As I spoke, I unpacked my lunch, and though Margaret listened intently, I saw that she was making an effort not to look at the sandwiches. The smell of fresh bread, ham, and pickles made my mouth water. For the first time, I noticed how very thin Margaret was.

"Oh, no, not again," I said, gazing at my lunch.

"What is it?"

"Our cook always gives me too much lunch. She thinks I'm too thin. If I don't finish, I'll get into trouble again. I always seem to be in trouble of some kind. I don't try to, really I don't. Well . . . it just seems to come naturally."

Margaret laughed. "I understand. You know I was your age once, too."

"Margaret?"

"Yes, Brigitte?"

"Would you help me finish my lunch?"

Margaret almost lowered her eyes but then held them steady. She shook her head. "Well, no thank you, I really couldn't."

"The trouble is I sneaked some cake this morning," I fibbed. "I don't have much of an appetite. I'll catch the devil if I don't finish this lunch."

Margaret smiled faintly, a knowing yet faintly embarrassed look on her face.

"All right, Brigitte, I will share your lunch with you."

Fifteen years later, standing in a strange village in the cold drizzle, watching this woman eat, I realized something I had never known. The important part of that experience wasn't my giving Margaret a sandwich but my offering it to her in a way that enabled her to accept it.

Now the woman turned her head and stared out at me. She opened her window.

"Are you hungry?" she asked me.

I nodded.

The woman looked at me, her face blank. During those initial weeks of occupation, people seldom expressed emotions. "Here," she said. She picked up the half loaf of bread and handed it to me.

I took it. *So this is begging*, I thought. *First, I became a thief, now I've become a beggar.* I did not feel gratitude. I felt nothing. I just stared at her in a kind of trance. She did not look like Margaret. She was younger, and her face, though thin, was not emaciated as Margaret's had been. Yet I felt that she *was* Margaret. In some strange way, it was Margaret who had reached through the window and placed bread in my hand. I kept walking.

That night, I took shelter from the rain in a barn where half a dozen German refugees were huddled. It wasn't long before the wife of the farmer, wielding a pitchfork, drove us out, shouting, "Out! Out! Lice! Lice!" She drove us into the cattle yard. Light from a kerosene lamp she held made her face look inhuman under the rubber rain hat. A part of me sympathized with her. Streams of refugees from liberated labor factories were moving eastward across the countryside, many of them infested with lice. If they could get a change of clothes, they would abandon their old ones on the spot. Often, I came upon piles of castoff clothes, crawling with lice, the stench rising. I walked away from the barn and only when I got to the road did I realize that I had left my shoes behind me. I did not return for them. My feet had terrible blisters. I thought that maybe the shoes had caused the blisters. I didn't think that walking barefoot could be more painful than walking in those stiff shoes.

Later that night the rain stopped, the temperature dropped to near freezing. The only way I could stay somewhat warm was to keep moving. I walked most of that night and all the next day, asking people in villages if they had seen three persons together, a boy of Alex's description, a woman, and a little girl. Not one person I asked could help me. That evening, believing I could not stand another night in the woods in the cold, I stopped at a farmhouse. An old woman answered my knock. Her eyes were angry and fearful. I asked if I could sleep on her floor. She hesitated. Then the fear and anger in her eyes were replaced with weariness.

"All right," she said. It seemed that it wasn't sympathy for me but a kind of resigned weariness that prompted her answer. She brought me two horse blankets and said, "I'll show you to the barn." As we walked behind the house, she lighting the way with a kerosene lamp, we came upon two German soldiers. They seemed to be in their early teens. Around the sleeves of their oversized uniforms were Red Cross armbands. The boys were weeping. German, boy soldiers, seeming to materialize out of nowhere, weeping in the middle of a barnyard . . . it was just another uncommon scene in a world gone mad.

The appearance of the boys did not surprise the woman. She sighed heavily. "So young. Both of you are too young to be soldiers. Where are you from? Where are you going?"

"What does it matter?" I said. "Couldn't they stay in the barn with me?"

"I'll bring more blankets," she said and walked back to the house.

As soon as I lay down in the barn, I fell asleep. But the sound of Russians speaking in broken German at the house woke me. "Women . . . where . . . take . . . barn . . . ."

Their footsteps splashed across the yard in the mud. The barn door rattled violently open. The woman's lantern threw feeble light inside. I saw two dark shapes looming beside her before I covered my head with the blanket.

"Women? . . . " A soldier asked.

"Boys, only boys," the woman said.

The Russians began conversing with each other. One of the boys, lying beside me under the horse blanket, began trembling, trembling with increased intensity as the Russians spoke with each other.

Then the door rattled shut. Darkness engulfed us again. The footsteps went back to the house.

The next day I left the boys sleeping in the barn and knocked on the woman's door, wanting to thank her. But she did not answer. Hoping the Russians hadn't taken her, I left the rolled-up horse blankets on the doorstep and set out again on the highway.

That afternoon I entered a large town and went to the town clerk's office where some fifty refugees had queued in the street for ration cards. I went to the head of the queue and asked the old woman clerk if she had registered a woman, with a young boy and girl, for food stamps. It was a question I had asked many times in many towns and villages. I expected to be answered "no" this time, too, as the woman ran her finger down names in a registry book; but instead she spoke words that sent an electric shock through me. "Yes, here they are. A woman and two small children. Staying with a family in town." I hurried to the address she gave me, laughing out loud yet also close to tears. I couldn't believe it. Alex was here. After weeks of searching I had found him. I thought of his sunny face and wondered how he would greet me. At the address I was given, a sweet-looking, elderly woman opened the door. "Yes, may I help you?"

Breathless, I said, "The clerk in town told me that you have my son here."

"How wonderful! He's been such a good little boy. Please come in. I'll get him."

I was trembling with relief and happiness when she came back, holding the hand of a darling little boy—a boy who was not Alex.

"You're not my mommy," he said angrily and tearfully.

"No?" The woman looked at me.

I shook my head.

"Oh, I am sorry."

I thanked her and walked from the house. To have my expectations raised then dashed felt so much worse than all the "no's" I had heard in all the days before. I tried to convince myself that finding this one little boy was a good sign. If I could find someone else's child, then I could certainly find my own. But I also knew that my deep disappointment prompted me for the first time to think that I may not ever find Alex—not because he couldn't be found but because I wasn't smart, strong, or resourceful enough to do it by myself.

9

A Little Bit of Kindness

ONE MORNING, the procession of refugees shuffling westward slowly came to a halt. For hours, I stayed in one place. It was bad enough being a refugee on the move; but when we stopped and did not move again I felt as if I had been thrown into a cramped pit. Around me stood a sea of old men and women, of women and their children. Word came down through the long lines of people that the Russians had blocked the road and were letting only a small number of refugees into the American sector. Gradually, I understood that I was in one long queue. Fearful of losing their places in line, the refugees urinated and defecated right beside the road, creating cesspools—rank enough where I was but, no doubt, up ahead where people had been waiting for a longer period of time, much worse. I knew that resourceful Greta, whom I thought was trying to cross into the American sector, would not sit in this line with the children, subjecting them to disease. So I decided to double-back and keep searching in the Russian sector.

To keep away from the Russians, I not only avoided the main roads but side roads too, hiding in woods at night when enemy soldiers were particularly active in their search for women. One late afternoon, I found myself wandering lost in deep, pine woods. Because I had eaten only a few pieces of bread in several days and had become sick from drinking bad water, I began hallucinating. I saw a tree expand and contract as if it were breathing . . . a moss-covered boulder get up on four clawed feet and walk like a turtle . . . a brook of clear water turn to blood and the stones in the blood become broken bones.

Yet in my confused state, the hallucinations did not terrify me. I had been through these kind of magical woods before. Margaret had taken me through them that special summer fifteen years earlier. We met many times after I shared my lunch with her on the park bench. Even my brother Pott, who was two years younger than I and always on the go, never sitting still, joined us in our afternoon get-togethers on the bench. Pott and I would pack lunches, slipping in extra sandwiches and sweets for Margaret.

Margaret told us wonderful stories, of knights and princesses and magical forests. I asked her where she had learned of such wonderful people and places. "My godfathers wrote fairy tales," she answered. "When I was a little girl, I would spend hours with them. I think I was their testing ground. If I liked the story, they would write it down."

"And you're my godmother," I said and leaped up from the grass where I had been lying with Pott, listening. I hugged her and said, "You're our fairy godmother, isn't she Pott?" Pott nodded his head in agreement.

After walking in a kind of delirium for the good part of a day, I came upon a thatched-roofed stone house that stood in a small clearing. The sun was setting, illuminating only the tops of trees, while the house and forest floor fell into deep shadows. I was not sure whether this ethereal scene was real or another of my hallucinations.

I crossed a dirt road and knocked on the wood and iron door. There was no answer. I suddenly realized that moving across the road and knocking on the door without knowing for sure who might be there was a stupid mistake. I thought of sprinting back into the woods. Then the door opened. I stood there, trembling and holding my breath.

A tall, broad-shouldered, old man stood at the threshold. For the first time in weeks or months I was staring into the face of a German who was not frightened, dazed, or in pain. I was dirty, barefoot, and mad looking, but he looked at me sympathetically with very sad eyes.

"Have Russians been here?" I asked.

"No. No one has been here. And no one is likely to come by either. The inn is isolated. You look exhausted. Please come in."

I sat at a table by a window that looked out onto a small patio garden.

"You look hungry," he said. "May I offer you some food? Maybe a bed for the night? There isn't much, but what I have is yours."

The next thing I knew I was lying on the floor and the old man was gently shaking my shoulders.

"What happened?"

"I think you fainted. Are you well enough to get up and eat a little something?"

"Yes."

He served me warm broth and boiled potato soup. The first spoonful erupted like a miracle in my mouth. At that moment, it was the most delicious soup I had ever tasted. After eating soup and bread, I washed up as best I could with a basin of water, then sat in front of blazing logs in the fireplace and told the old man about my search. He sat on the edge of a chair, elbows on his knees, and listened intently as I told him about losing my son and my unsuccessful attempts to find him during the past weeks. He said he would help me any way he could, but first I should get a night's rest. He showed me to a guest room. He never asked for payment for the food, the bath, or the bed. I knew that for the first time in weeks, I could sleep for a night and not suffer cold or be afraid.

But those were the days when knowledge and plans meant nothing, when the only reality was survival. I had slept for several hours when I was awakened by Russian voices. Nothing surprised me in those days. I just lived on and did what the moment asked and needed of me. I put on my clothes—those dirty, torn, rank clothes were priceless possessions—and tip-toed to the window. It sounded as if there were three or four soldiers downstairs. They were speaking drunkenly, laughing, singing snatches of songs, throwing things about. I opened the window carefully. It was a one-story drop to the ground. If the Russians came upstairs and found me, they would probably kill the old man for not saying that I was here, and heaven only knew what they would do to me. I felt I had only one chance to save both of us. If they found no one in the house, they would probably not harm him. Hoping that the noise of my landing would not be heard, I jumped. I landed in bushes, my heart drumming in my ears. I did not notice I was limping and that pain was searing my ankle until I had gotten far away from the house into deeper woods.

10

A Brush with Madness and Death

I DID NOT KNOW if my ankle was broken or badly sprained. Although it swelled considerably, the swelling was not as noticeable as it might have been because, during the past weeks, as I gorged on brook water to ease hunger pains, my body had become very bloated. I discovered a bizarre way to pass the time: Pressing my finger into the skin on my bloated arms, I counted the seconds until the dimple popped up and the skin became even again. I repeated this strange ritual over and over.

I knew I could not merely continue to wander the woods. If I were to find Alex, I had to come out in the open. I had to spend more time searching in towns.

My ankle remained painfully swollen, but the blisters on my feet healed and calluses formed. A German soldier, who had discarded his uniform and whose ragged, filthy clothes made him resemble an animated scarecrow as he marched swiftly along the road, told me that bathing my feet regularly in cold brook water would harden the skin.

"My troops spent three months marching in subzero weather in Russia," he said. "Our shoes and socks wore out, and finally we ended up marching barefoot. First came the blisters, then the infection, then the frostbite, and then some lost their toes and feet. If you wash your feet morning, noon, and night in the cold water, it will help harden the skin and callouses will form. Before long, you won't mind the road or the cold so much."

He said no more and went marching off ahead of me, working out his own particular survival. I took his advice. The cold water treatment helped, and as my feet hardened, I could cover a greater distance.

I had gotten to the point where almost every little boy in every town I went to looked like Alex. I could not leave a town without having to go back and scrutinize the children in the streets again—then go back again and again to the same streets, the same children.

But what was worse than my seeing Alex in so many little boys, was my thinking that I might come upon him and not recognize him. I knew that every day I did not find him increased the chances that he would become a stranger to me. A young child changes so much, month to month, even week to week. The changes that took place in war could be more enduring and devastating than those happening in normal times. So, I repeatedly returned to the same children I had looked at carefully, thinking that a certain little boy *must* be Alex, only to finally tell myself that of course he wasn't Alex—but, when I walked away, I was tormented by the thought that he really *was* Alex, and that if I continued to walk away, I would never see him again.

A Brush with Madness and Death

One day in a side street of a village, I found myself clutching Alex, weeping with joy, crying, "Alex, Alex, I found you." Alex was squirming in my arms, and I only held him more tightly, never wanting to let him go again. "Don't cry, Alex, it's Mommy!"

A burly woman ran up to me.

"Put my son down!" She clawed my arms away from Alex.

I didn't understand. Why was she trying to separate me from Alex? Alex was crying, reaching toward the woman. "Mommy! Mommy! Mommy!" he shouted.

I came out of my trance. This wasn't Alex in my arms. It was a strange little boy.

I let him go. He rushed into his mother's arms.

I backed away from them, clutching my head. "I'm sorry. I'm sorry."

I hurried from the village, knowing that I was beginning to lose my mind. Yet madness wasn't frightening. Instead, it beckoned as a kind of liberation. When I held the boy, a part of me knew that he really wasn't Alex. Yet another part of me enjoyed the delusion. I realized that the most dangerous part of madness wasn't the delusion but my enjoyment of it. I knew that if I gave in to it, it would be Alex who would ultimately suffer; Alex who would be lost forever.

My search took me to the Mulde River. Here the Americans were on the east, not the west bank. The river was running high and dark brown, with logs, saplings, and war wreckage floating slowly downstream. A railroad bridge that had spanned the river had been blown up and the bridge's twisted girders and shattered stone pilings stuck up out of the waters. Rain gusted across this dismal scene.

Across the river was a village where old friends lived, friends who might have seen or heard of Alex. I had to somehow cross the river and find out. I couldn't swim directly across. The current would carry me far downstream. So I walked upriver for several hundred yards, looking for a safe place to enter the water. A halftrack American reconnaissance vehicle came grinding along a muddy path that paralleled the river, one American soldier behind a big machine gun in the back of the vehicle, two Americans in front. The man on the passenger's side shouted at me and swung his arm, beckoning. I walked to the vehicle. The soldier spoke English, or something that sounded like English, but not quite the way Winifred, our English governess, had spoken it. She had spoken such phrases as, "Hold your tongues, children," or "In a fortnight," and "Rather!. . ." It was not this nasal, choppy kind of English at all. But I understood well enough to know that I wasn't permitted in this area. I nodded and walked away from the river. But, when the vehicle disappeared downriver behind some willows, I turned back around and headed to the water's edge. I didn't want to get my shirt and trousers soaked, so I took them off, bundled them up, and held them over my head as I began to wade into the river. "Now or never," I said.

The cold water numbed me, sapping what little strength I had. I had for years been a strong swimmer. I loved athletics, especially, riding, skiing, swimming, gymnastics, and track. (In fact, I had even been an alternate for the 1936 Olympics in the women's high jump.) My years of engaging in rigorous athletics saved me. In the strong, cold current, I nearly lost consciousness and had to draw on reserves of strength I did not know I had. Just before the current swept me into the wreckage of the bridge, I floundered ashore. I crawled into some shrubs that were just beginning to leaf, which provided some screening, and put on my clothes. I crawled through sandy mud to the edge of the shrubs and peered at the village. Seeing no sign of troops, I climbed out, and headed towards my friends' house.

The last time I had seen them, they lived in a large, marble-block house by the river. Now the windows were boarded up, and the door was nailed shut. I went behind the house to the servants' quarters where rain water, pouring through broken roof gutters above me, cascaded onto the cobblestones. Shutters were pulled across the windows, but through the space between the shutters I could see a light burning inside. I knocked on the door. No one answered. I knocked again. Finally, a voice behind the door said suspiciously, "Who is it?"

I recognized Clara's voice. "Clara," I called out. "It's me. It's Brigitte."

The door opened. Clara stood there. I had not seen her since the previous year when Alex and I had visited the house on our way to Dresden.

A stocky, middle-aged woman looked at me and did not recognize me. She was on the verge of flinging the door shut.

"I'm Brigitte," I said. She narrowed her eyes and then ran them up and down my clothes.

"Oh, yes, hello, Brigitte," she answered sourly. "What are you doing here?"

She did not invite me in, but I stepped inside anyway, into a low-ceilinged room lit by two kerosene lamps. A coal fire burned in a cheap cast iron stove. At the far end of the room, wearing suspenders and a woolen undershirt, a dour, dark-faced man sat in a wheelchair at a table, eating what looked like potato soup. This was Clara's husband, a veterinarian. He had been wounded in France and confined to a wheelchair at the outbreak of the war. Though he recognized me, he greeted me only with a curt nod of his head.

I wondered why they decided to live in the servant's quarters. Perhaps it was because they wanted to be unnoticed by the Communists.

"What brings you here?" Clara said. "Where have you been? What is it you want?" She spoke mechanically. Clearly, neither she nor her husband were happy to see me.

I asked if they had seen Alex.

Her husband, chewing a potato, shook his head.

"We don't know anything about your son," Clara said. "Look, you're making a mess on the floor with your wet clothes."

I looked down at the small puddle of brown water collecting around my bare feet. "Sorry I troubled you," I said, not wanting to show how hurt, embarrassed, and angry I was, and turned on my heel and left.

I went back to the river and walked upstream. An old man standing in the yard of a stone cottage shouted for me to be careful because Russian and American troops along the river banks were arresting Germans as spies. I thanked him and waved and then crawled into and through the shrubs until I got a clear view of the far river bank. I saw no troops nor vehicles where I intended to come out of the water. So I removed my clothes and went into the river once again—and again I miscalculated the current's power. It nearly swept me into the bridge abutments. I crawled up the riverbank, staying in the brush and under the overhang of the bank. When I got to the top of the riverbank, a pair of boots blocked my path.

I looked up. An American soldier was standing there, rain pelting his rubber poncho. He was the same soldier who had warned me away from the river several hours before. I could not understand where he had come from. I had entered the water only when I saw that this side of the river was clear. He told me to get dressed and, in a display of civility that seemed incongruous in that time of rape and brutality, turned his back on me while I put on my clothes. When I was dressed, he turned around and began screaming at me and gesturing angrily. Piecing together what English phrases I could understand, I realized that I was being arrested.

As he led me around the bridge abutment, I understood why I had not seen him. His vehicle had been stuck in swampy grass behind the downstream side of the abutment. He had watched me cross the river and had been waiting for me.

When we reached his vehicle, four other American soldiers were in the process of pushing it free, the steel tracks spitting liquid mud and grass. Finally, the halftrack backed up onto firmer ground. The American ordered me to come along. Was I going to jail? Would I be tried as a spy as the old man had warned? I grasped a handgrip and tried to pull myself up onto the halftrack's metal plates, but my feet slipped in the mud and I fell to my knees. One of the Americans shoved his hands under my arms and lifted me in the air and set me down on the steel floor. Under the rumbling of the engine, I heard a faint hissing. The metal plates, heated by the friction of the spinning tracks, were burning the soles of my feet. The hissing was the sound of my skin burning. I stifled a cry of pain. The soldier at the machine gun threw oily rags on top of the plates.

"Stand on those," he ordered. A glimmer of sympathy shone through his dirty, combat-hardened face.

It was getting dark when we pulled into town. Suddenly, the halftrack stopped and one of the soldiers pushed me onto the street. The vehicle sped off into the dark. I sat up in the street, bewildered. I didn't understand why they hadn't locked me up. They arrested me, why hadn't they put me in jail? Maybe they didn't want to deal with the consequences of my having burned my feet. Maybe they thought I would be picked up by MPs enforcing curfew. I rolled onto my hands and knees. I tried to stand up, but the pain in my feet ripped through them like knives, and I had to sit back down. A cold wind was blowing sheets of rain down the street. The prospect of spending another night in the cold loomed again. I felt as if a great blackness were swallowing me. I was in a state of mental and physical collapse. After weeks of patiently waiting for my feet to heal, of trying not to aggravate my injured ankle, I had injured my feet once again. I had to go back to crawling on hands and knees. A few weeks earlier, when my blisters had become so very painful, I spent several days when it was almost easier to crawl than walk. But the blisters had healed, and recently I had been able to walk sixty kilometers a day—measuring my progress by counting the stone markers on the side of the highways. But now I did not know if I had the strength to continue my search and heal once again.

I was living just moment to moment. There was no tomorrow for me now. There was not even a tonight. There was only now. And the next now I moved into. On hands and knees, I made my way into what I recognized as a *Schräbergarten*, a complex of tiny gardens owned and tended by people from urban areas. Of course, nobody was tending the gardens these days. But they seemed to hold a kind of haven. Ahead of me, there was a small, wooden garden shed. I found the handle of a discarded hoe and pushed the end of the handle against a door latch. The door swung open and I crawled inside. A male's voice spoke in the darkness: "Who have we here?"

I bit my lip to stifle a moan of fear. *Oh, Alex*, I thought, waiting to be shot or clubbed in the dark. *I'm so sorry. I tried so hard. And failed so miserably.*

The voice said: "I'll get her. Hurry up. You close the door."

11

Angels in a Shed

THAT NIGHT I WAS VISITED by angels. Instead of halos and white robes, they wore beards and dirty, rain-soaked clothes, but they were angels nevertheless.

I was pulled inside, the door closed, and somebody lit a candle. I saw three men in a small, cramped space, all dressed in rags. Their bearded faces resembled the faces of Biblical prophets. Yet there was something strangely young about their faces, too, as if they were boys transformed into old men by the war. One of them ripped the sleeves of one of several shirts he wore into strips, and bandaged my feet. Another pulled four pieces of bread from deep inside his rags. The third removed an oilcloth package from his pocket and unwrapped strings of magnificent, cooked sausages. We shared the bread and sausages. No longer afraid, I told them of my plight. Then one said that I looked very tired and ought to sleep. I think those were the first and only words spoken to me in that shed. When I awoke in the morning, the angels had vanished. The bandages were on my feet. Two large pieces of bread, sausages, and a canteen of water lay by my side. I believed then and I believe today that those men truly were from heaven.

I stayed in the garden shed for two days, keeping off my feet, which were badly swollen but not infected. On the third day, I began my search again.

But after several days of being back on the road, hobbling through a village, I felt an excruciating pain stab my stomach. I doubled over on the side of the road and lay there in terrible pain before two old women helped me to my feet. They took me to their cottage and gave me black tea to drink. The tea helped ease the pain a little. Before long, however, it returned with renewed intensity; and it became obvious that I needed medical attention right away. The hospital was only a short distance away, and the two women helped me on my painful walk. The doctor examined me and said that I had colic of the gallbladder. I was medicated, and I spent the night there. In the morning, I explained that I could not stay because I had no money to pay them. The doctor said that I was well enough to go on.

Then followed days of nightmarish walking, searching, questioning, sleeping in ditches at night, getting up in the dark of the morning, teeth rattling, shivering, clothes stiff with frozen dew, walking to warm up, having nothing warm to drink, begging for food, rushing to every four-year-old blue-eyed boy I saw, knocking on doors, getting addresses of orphaned children, looking them up, and never finding Alex.

My discouragement became so overwhelming that even just asking about Alex, just getting the words out of my mouth, became almost more than I could bear. I would knock on the door of an address I had been given, a woman would open the door, and then I would stand there, speechless. I thought that if I didn't ask, she couldn't say no. Standing before her, I could imagine her saying, "Yes, yes, he's here. He's been such a good boy. He told me every day that his Mommy was on her way, and here you are." But it was only a fantasy I had created, a way to keep myself going. Finally, when I did ask, and received the usual "no," the dose of reality was almost too much to take, and I would walk away so depressed I could hardly breathe.

My searching was taking place in a land overrun by the Russians and Americans, where German women, young and old, were the targets of rape, and where many women often ended their misery by taking the lives of their children and then their own. Shortly after I left the hospital, I began to realize that I was running out of strength and out of the power to focus on finding Alex. When I first set out on my search, I did not think about time. I knew that I would keep searching until I found him. As long as I could find food, I could go on. But through my exhaustion and confusion filtered the realization that I must find him very, very soon, or I would no longer have the strength to keep searching.

Aware at last that I needed help, I thought of the only person who could help. My mother.

12

My Mother

I REMEMBERED MY MOTHER HAD SAID that she was going to find her mother in Chemnitz. I had heard, however, shortly after Dresden had been bombed, that Chemnitz had been hit by a large attack, too. I thought that Mother had probably taken Grandmother to my aunt's house in Grossenhain.

Grossenhain was many kilometers away, and a hard walk, too. In a way, I did not want to get there. I did not want to make another wrong decision. I was afraid that if she were not there, and I could not get any leads as to where she was, that I may have to give up my search until I somehow could regain my strength and rationality. For I did not know if I could again recover from another mistake or wrong choice.

When I reached Grossenhain, I walked beside a canal and looked over the iron rail. I watched my reflection in the water and recalled the last time I had been there, a few years earlier, and saw the same canal, the same rail. Back then children played beside the canal under oak trees. I remembered, too, the lake near the canal and how, one time, my uncle (a wonderful and distinguished gentleman) and my older brother were about to go sailing, and how my uncle pushed the boat away from the dock but did not let go of the stern and found himself stretched between stern and dock before plunging into the water. My mother, father, and I, standing on the dock, laughed hysterically over that comic splash. Later we laughed again when my uncle's wife arrived in the car to pick up my dripping wet, not-so-distinguished-looking uncle.

I had so many happy times in Grossenhain; and now I walked here, unrecognizable, dirty, bloated, wretched in my filthy clothes with my features deformed by the beret that I had worn for more than two months.

My aunt and uncle's house stood beside a brook. Boards were nailed across the front door. I pushed my thumb against the button for the electric bell, but no sound came from inside. Either the bell was broken or there was no electricity. I knocked but no one answered. Calling, "Hello, hello, hello," I walked down flagstone steps beside the house toward the brook, knowing that my mother wasn't there, that I had been wrong again, calling out now not for my mother, but just to see if any living person was in that house.

A first-floor window opened. A woman looked out. She looked right into my eyes, fearfully, suspiciously. She said, "Can I help you?"

Staring at her, I couldn't speak. I was looking right at my mother. I couldn't move. She didn't recognize me. I was close enough to touch her. But my mother didn't recognize me. Had I become somebody else? Had I finally lost my mind?

My Mother

"Just a moment, please," she said, speaking in that distant way she would speak to a stranger. She turned around and took two steps away from the window. I did not know where she was going, or what her intention was.

It was then that she must have realized who I was. She screamed.

She called out the nickname she had given to me when I was a child. "Mäusi! Mäusi!" It meant "little mouse." She hadn't called me that name in years.

I ran around to the back door; she opened it and we embraced and sobbed and sobbed—awful, awful sobbing, but sobbing that was also a kind of release.

At last, when she composed herself, she led me inside. I looked for toys on the floor or a little shoe, or something that would indicate that a child was living there. But no child's things were in sight.

"Mäusi, sit down. You look awful. It breaks my heart that I didn't recognize you."

In a choked voice, I asked, "Mutti, is Alex here?"

"Alex?" she said. "Oh, my God, no. Where is he?"

"I don't know. We became separated two months ago. I haven't been able to find him."

"God help us, Brix!" She pressed her hands to her face and sat there, motionless. I knew she was thinking, planning, just as she had planned in the basement during the bombing of Dresden. Finally, she dropped her hands and said, "I will go with you. There's no other choice. We both have to search for him. Don't worry. We're together. We'll search for him together."

I leaned against my mother. She rocked me gently, kissing my forehead, holding me for dear life. Finally, I slept.

13

On to Leipzig

SECURE IN MY MOTHER'S CARE, I slept for a day and a night, then part of another day. I awoke to find my mother sitting next to me on the bed.

"How long have I slept?"

"A day and a half. I was going to let you sleep longer, but I thought you would want to get going again."

"But where can I go? It seems I've been everywhere. And yet I really have been nowhere. I don't know what to do anymore."

"We've got to think this through," my mother said.

We sat at the kitchen table, and she led me step by step through my journey. Through her prompting, I told her that Greta had given me an address in Leipzig. It was an easy address to remember, but I couldn't imagine how Greta could have gotten through the American and Russian lines and made it there.

"I'm sure I was close behind her. I know what roadblocks she probably faced. I faced them, too. She couldn't have gotten through them."

"She might have made it. Look how far you've come."

She was right. During the months of my panicky searching, I never thought that Greta could have made it through. She had two children with her and would surely have been stopped. So I had stayed in the same area. But, talking to my mother, I remembered how resourceful Greta was. She could very well have made the longer, more difficult trek to Leipzig. "Leipzig's a long shot," I said, "But I think we should try it."

"Let's leave right away," she said. "Russian soldiers stay in this house often. They've knocked down the door so many times, I finally decided to board it up. I come and go through the window. When they come, we'll probably have to give them all our food. And then we'll have to stay as long as they're here. They haven't hurt me, but some of them are primitive. One group used the sink for a toilet and the toilet for a sink. There's no telling what the next group might do. Let's pack now."

She supervised our packing, putting clothes into a rucksack and a small, leather traincase. She found an old-fashioned, light green perambulator; we put the suitcase and rucksack inside and set off.

We weren't more than several kilometers down the road outside of town towards Leipzig when we heard a truck approaching behind us. I knew that meant only one thing. No Germans had trucks then.

"Mother, Russians!" In an instant, I realized we had made a mistake taking the pram. It meant that we had to stay on roads. When traveling alone, I could move like a shadow where and when I wanted. It had been my mother's decision to take the pram, and I realized that she had no idea what kind of world we were entering.

I was aware that, for the first time in my life, it was I who had to lead my mother and that her safety depended, to a great extent, on my knowledge and resourcefulness.

As the truck approached, I experienced that lightheaded, trembling hysteria that had accompanied all my wrong decisions during the past months.

"Look down," I told my mother. "Don't look at them."

The truck came alongside us and slowed, moving along at our speed. Then it pulled a little ahead of us and stopped.

A Russian, speaking in broken German, asked where we were going. Keeping my eyes on my feet, I raised a shaky finger and pointed down the road. Slowly, we came up alongside the truck.

To my horror, the Russian climbed down from the cab and stood in front of us, blocking our way. I looked at his muddy boots, avoiding his eyes. Without speaking, he took the rucksack out of the pram and handed it to me and took the traincase out and gave it to my mother. He kicked the pram into the ditch, then gestured for me to get into the truck.

I sneaked a look at his face. It was a young boy's face, pock-marked, with black, strangely beautiful eyes.

"Go on," Mother said. "He's offering us a ride."

"Don't trust him. He'll kill us. I've seen things. I know."

Shrugging my shoulders I lifted my hands as if I did not understand what he was saying. He grabbed my arm and led me around the side of the truck. He gestured for me to get into the back. I was so afraid that I hardly had the strength to climb inside. He hopped onto the back and held out his hand. I took it, and he helped the two of us up. Then he went around and got into the cab. With the rattling of a motor badly in need of an overhaul, the truck drove off.

Scattered about us under a greasy, flapping canvas roof were spare engine parts, puddles of motor oil, potato peelings, several beat-up boots, bloody chicken feathers, empty shell casings, an ornate table lamp, horseshoes, and a big, brass cash register. Mother was as frightened as I was; and sitting there in hiking clothes, hugging her knees, her eyes shut tightly, she was praying, praying with fierce determination. I too prayed and also thought of leaping off and dragging her with me. But even if we could have gotten off without the Russians seeing us, even if we wouldn't have been injured landing on the asphalt, we were in open country; there was no place to hide. Through a little glass window, I could see into the cab and out the front of the truck. As we drove toward a village crossroads, I knew I had one chance. I knocked on the cab window. The soldier turned around and stared at me through the glass.

"Here! Off! Off!" I shouted.

The truck stopped. The soldier got out and came around to the back. "*Hier? Hier?*" he asked.

I nodded. He helped me from the back. Then he reached out toward my mother. He lifted her gently off the back and set her down.

"*Auf Wiedersehen,*" he said, with a thick Russian accent.

He got into the cab, and drove a little ways down

On to Leipzig

the road before I understood what had happened: A Russian, instead of harming us, had actually helped us, actually wanted to help us.

It took us nearly a week to walk to Leipzig. On the outskirts, we came upon a roadblock set up by American soldiers. I told them that we had been driven out of the city during the war and now were coming back to our home. I said that my son was there, and as soon as we got him, we would head on to my husband's home in Garmisch. It was a plausible story, and we were let through.

We arrived at the address Greta had given me. It was a small house near the industrial outskirts of the city. The door opened after I knocked only once. There stood Greta. Her broad face looked older and thinner; the clear, confident gaze she had when I met her in the castle was clouded. Apparently, she had been through an ordeal as well. "Is Alex here?" I immediately asked, fighting back a feeling of panic.

She gave me a strange look. "Come in and sit down," she said.

Mother and I walked inside. There were just a few sticks of furniture in the room and a mattress with a blanket on it.

"I don't want to sit down," I said. "I want to know where Alex is."

"He's safe."

"Thank God," my mother said.

"But where is he?" I demanded. My panic had given way to anger.

Greta told us of the two days that she had waited for me to return to the castle. Refugees coming and going kept warning her that the Russians were on their way. "I couldn't wait any longer. I had to take Alex and Margot and leave. Where were you?" The question was almost an accusation.

"The Russians had come into Dresden and locked me up. I got back as soon as I could." I tried to keep my expression calm to conceal my growing anger. I wanted to avoid an argument with her. My overriding objective was to get all the details about Alex.

"You have no idea what we faced on our trek here."

"I have an idea. I would have come to Leipzig right away, but I didn't think that you could be that far ahead of me. I thought that I could catch up with you. What I didn't know then was that there was no way we could have found each other. Alex . . . where is Alex?"

Greta gave me that strange look again. She took a piece of paper from a desk drawer. She put the paper in my hand. "This is where I left Alex. I would have kept him with me, but it was too much for me to take care of both children. I am also pregnant."

I took the piece of paper and thanked her.

"I hope that he's still there. I don't know what I would do if I lost Margot."

"But you didn't lose Margot."

She shook her head. "No, I didn't." She was silent for a moment, then she said, "I'm sorry that I didn't do a better job of watching him. I did try, Brigitte."

"I know you did. I entrusted him to you, and I have no regrets about that. It's been a nightmare for all of us."

She hugged me and whispered in my ear, "I'm so sorry."

I nodded. Mother took her hand and shook it and said, "I know that you did the best you could. Now let's pray that Alex is still there. I don't think my daughter can hold on much longer."

We left her house and once more started our search. The address sent us eastward again.

14

Chasing Another Lead

FOLLOWING GRETA'S DIRECTIONS, we walked until we reached a bridge that crossed a small river. It looked like so many bridges I had encountered in my search for Alex. As I crossed each one, I dared to hope that my son was waiting on the other side. *Was this just another bridge like all the others?* I wondered.

My mother and I approached a lanky American soldier who, with a carbine slung on his back, stood outside a guard house. When he spotted us, I saw his expression harden. He turned his back on us and gazed past the narrow, wooden bridge that crossed the river beside him. On the other side of the bridge, there was a similar guard house with a Russian soldier standing beside it. Beyond the Russian guard house was a village.

"Please . . ." I said to the American. "Please . . . may I talk to you? I can speak English."

Reluctantly, he turned back around. I saw that hatred toward Germans, so common in the faces of Americans, Russians, and Poles, twist the corners of his mouth. I knew that he would not listen to me. He would not

Another Bridge

want to help even if he did listen. I remembered my first encounter with Americans, getting arrested, burning my feet, getting pushed out of the reconnaissance vehicle in the village. But I also remembered the American turning his back while I got dressed and the other American who threw rags on the hot floorplates, so I took heart and spoke.

As I told him my story, fearfully, hopefully, the story I had repeated hundreds of times during the past three months, "I'm a mother who has lost her child . . . ," I saw his mouth twist even more. Then he looked away and breathed deeply in a show of exasperation. "I have been told that my son might be in a house in that village across the river. May I cross that bridge and see?"

He removed his helmet and wiped beads of perspiration from his forehead. It was a sunny day, and his brown shirt was dark with sweat. In the moment that he drew his sleeve across his face, I knew that he was making a decision—trifling for him but potentially shattering for me.

"Wait," he said and walked into the guard house.

He came out with an officer who was clean, well fed, and boyish looking. A single silver bar glistened on his collar.

Mechanically, I repeated, "I am a mother. I have lost my child. . . ."

The officer listened, running his eyes up and down me, then up and down my mother. He showed no hatred. Instead, he actually seemed to be pondering my story. While I talked, a part of me thought, *He's so clean, so young, so human.*

He gave me a doubtful look then said, "Do you have something to give? Gold? Jewelry?"

His request startled me. I hadn't expected this from an American. I looked at my mother. We badly needed that jewelry hidden in my trousers' cuffs as insurance for survival. She gave me a slight nod. I looked back at the officer. I wasn't ready to give up so easily. "Why do you ask?" I said. I tried to seem genuinely curious.

He lowered his gaze and rubbed his nose with the back of his slender hand. "I'm sorry. But it might be helpful."

"Yes," I said, trying not to let the anger in my voice be noticeable. "I have something to give."

"I'll be back," he said.

He walked across the bridge and entered the Russian guard house. My mother and I sat on the grassy bank and watched the guard house door. In those few minutes that seemed like hours, we decided between us that we would give up the ring with the diamond. As I waited, I felt my heart ache as it raced faster. Finally, the door opened; the American came out and walked back across the bridge. Time seemed to freeze. It seemed to take him forever to cross the bridge. I stood up, my face feeling cold and numb in the hot sun. The officer stopped at the end of the bridge and waved for me to come to him. I turned to my mother.

"Stay here," I said. "I'd better go alone. It's too dangerous for both of us."

She looked at me fearfully. We both knew that we were on a dangerous edge. When I walked off that edge, when I left her, we might not ever see each other again. "I love you," I told her. I stretched out my hand.

Tears came to her eyes. She clasped my hand and kissed it. "I love you, too," she said.

I turned from my mother and walked to the officer. It was like walking in a dream—like floating, not walking.

Another Bridge

"It's been arranged," he said. "The Russians say you can go to the address. But you have to have a Russian soldier accompany you. And you only have one hour."

"Only one hour?" I said and the emotion in my voice startled him. "I don't know if an hour is enough time."

"The Russians will be changing guards in an hour. The arrangement is only with the guards who are on duty now. You have to do what they say, or you can't do it at all."

I nodded. "I'll do it," I said.

"One more thing." He got that sad, embarrassed look again and wiped his nose with his hand. "The jewelry. You said you have jewelry."

I lifted my hand and uncurled my fingers. I had my fist closed so tightly that the diamond and my nails had made dents in the palm of my hand. He took the ring. "Come on. We don't have any time to lose."

He led me across the wood-planked bridge. Several times I glanced over my shoulder at my mother sitting on the bank, hugging her knees, watching me.

On the other side of the bridge, the American knocked on the guard house door. The door opened. I got a glimpse of four Russians at a table in their undershirts playing cards. The American went inside and shut the door.

Waiting, I remembered so many of the addresses I had walked to, and sometimes even crawled to, hoping that Alex would be there. Always, after being told no, I had found the strength to go on. But I began to wonder if I could recall how he truly looked. Not that he would have changed so much in three months, but that I had seen him in so many streets and yards and highways—

and yet had never seen him. Was my memory of him true to who he was or was that memory a composite of all the little boys I had recently seen?

A minute later, the American came out, followed by a tall, grim Russian soldier carrying a large rifle.

The American said, "Hurry. Give him the address. He'll take you there and bring you back. I'll wait on the other side of the bridge."

"Thank you," I said.

He nodded.

Without saying a word, without even acknowledging me, the Russian began walking toward the village. He went so swiftly that I had to take two steps to his one just to keep up with him. I wondered who had gotten the ring.

As we walked through the village, the soldier's boots clicking on the cobblestones, I tried to think of things other than the address we were going to and my hopes that Alex was there. Vivid memories came back to me. I remembered Margaret and the day that she didn't come to the park. On that day I found in the mailbox a flat, little box with many, tiny, intricate, paper flowers that had been carefully scissored, glued, and arranged. Enclosed with the flowers was a note from Margaret that said she she was going to visit her sister in Hamburg and had to move on before the summer ended. And I remembered how I cried because she was gone forever and had taken with her that final, special summer of my childhood. Walking behind the Russian, I also remembered my wedding night, skipping alongside Dieter, singing "Down Mexico way..." and how our trip to the Alps was another kind of end.

So, those memories of the end of youth and love had come to this moment as I followed an enemy soldier through a village to save my son, to save his youth, his love, his childhood.

It took all the strength I could muster to stay close to the soldier. I was not only tired, but afraid of him, too. Whether he knew it or not, he had ultimate power over me. He had my ring, or somebody else had my ring. He might think that I had more jewelry with me. He could take me anywhere and do anything he wanted with me.

We stopped at a stucco house on a muddy street on the outskirts of town. I walked up to the door and raised my hand to knock but couldn't bring it forward. I had sacrificed so much to come to this address, but now that I was here, I could not get up the courage to knock on the door. The weight of so many disappointments of the past three months crushed my spirit. I knew that if I experienced one more disappointment, I might not have any more strength to give to my son. Deal or no deal, time limit or no time limit, lost ring or no lost ring, I couldn't, could not bring myself to go through that door.

The soldier suddenly stamped his boot impatiently. He looked at the four wrist watches on his arm He pointed his rifle at me. "*Pascholl! Pascholl!*" I buried my face in my hands and shook my head. The Russian rapped angrily on the door with his rifle butt.

15

"No, My Son Is Not Here."

AN OLD WOMAN OPENED THE DOOR; and when she saw the Russian, she gasped, clutched her throat and went visibly pale. She was so frightened by the sudden and unexpected appearance of the soldier that she didn't see me standing beside him. When I spoke, she started again and looked at me incredulously.

"I'm a mother," I said. "I've lost my young son. This address was given to me, and I was told you took in a little boy for shelter."

The woman frowned and eyed me carefully. She stepped backward. "Come in."

With the low ceiling, the smoke blackened walls, and the tiny dusty windows letting in only dim light, I felt as if I were entering a cave. On the floor, four little children played. It was eerie. They did not make a sound. When we approached, they all looked at us. They were skinny. Their heads were partly shaved.

Another Bridge

They wore dark clothing and watched us silently, not moving. None of these children was my Alex, my blond, chubby, laughing Alex.

"No, my son is not here," I heard my voice say.

My disappointment was so great that my heart seemed to tear open. Still, I had known it would end this way. It always ended this way. It always would end this way. I would go on and on like this forever and never find him. How could I have ever expected to find him, a single, tiny child among hundreds of thousands of children, in this hell of defeat and occupation? I started to shake all over, and the old woman slipped her arms underneath mine, trying to steady me.

"I'm so sorry," she said.

"Thank you," I told the woman. I shook my head. I turned and started to leave.

"Mommy?"

The tiny voice behind me was hesitant, questioning, hopeful. I spun around and looked at the skinny, dirty-faced little boy who had uttered that word and was now standing and looking at me. He reached toward me, and I sank to my knees and gazed into his blue eyes. They were smiling with hope, yet a little fearful and near tears. I cupped his face in my hands and turned his head to glance behind his ears. There were the tiny scars from the mastoid operation he had had when he was six months old.

"Oh, my God, Alex, it is you!"

Shyly, he put his arms around my neck and whispered, "Mommy. Mommy."

"Alex, you knew me. You knew me!"

Tears running down my face, I held him tightly, his little body feeling so differently than I remembered. How much had he changed during the past months?

"No, My Son Is Not Here."

Who had Alex and I become? The answer would only be revealed to me in the months and years ahead. "It doesn't matter. It doesn't matter," I said aloud. "We're together. Nothing matters. Nothing at all now."

The Russian soldier coughed impatiently. I had forgotten all about him. I stood up with Alex in my arms. The soldier pointed to his watches. I realized that we had to return to the bridge right away or else we might never get out of the Russian zone. The woman brought a little, threadbare jacket for Alex to wear.

"How long have you cared for him?" I asked.

"Almost three months now. A woman left him here."

"Thank you. Thank you for my son."

The woman, tears in her eyes, embraced Alex and me. We went out of that oppressive dimness into bright sunlight, Alex riding piggy back. Trembling, I followed the Russian who walked swiftly on ahead.

"Mommy, Mommy, Mommy...." is all he said, his little legs and arms clinging fiercely to me.

"Oh, darling, I found you. Here we are together again. And we're going home. And you'll never be alone again."

At the bridge, I said goodbye to the Russian. I tried to put Alex down to shake the Russian's hand but Alex would not let go. I had to reach out and shake hands as best I could while still holding my son. The grim Russian looked at me from under his helmet, and, for the first time, he smiled. He shook my hand in a hearty, happy way. Then he waved.

As I started across the bridge, Alex said, "Mommy, I have to *kacke*."

The word startled me. He had never used such a word before. What kind of life had he lived for the past months for him to use that word? "Wait, darling. Wait until we get across the bridge."

I saw my mother. My mother had jumped to her feet and, waving frantically, she ran toward the bridge. She hadn't seen Alex since the bombing of Dresden.

"Alex, look, it's Ohmi! Remember Ohmi? See Ohmi?"

"Ohmi!" Alex shouted. His voice sounded so different from what I remembered. "Ohmi! Ohmi" He struggled free. He started to run toward the end of the bridge, his little, crude shoes stomping on the planks toward the West, toward freedom. Joyfully, I ran after him.

I knew even then that, although I had found him, a part of him was lost to me, and it would take months or years for us to find each other in our togetherness. But we had those months and years. As long as we were together, they would always be ours.

The American officer was waiting beside my mother. He was smiling, too.

16

November 1989

SHORTLY AFTER NOON, there is a knock on my office door. The tall man in the suit and tie opens it and peeks in. He smiles. "Remember our date, Mom? This morning you told me that we would have lunch together."

"Of course, Alex," I say. "I'm ready now."

Alex and I walk from the Consulate and down the street. We will have lunch together as we have done so many times over the years. We will talk about the latest United Way drive. We will talk about his children. We will talk about our jobs, his as a business executive, mine as Consul. But we will not talk about those three months that we were separated in 1945. He has never talked about that to me. Maybe he never will. Once, he told me that he remembered the Russian guard with the rifle who accompanied me into the house where I found him. But he did not say whether that is the only thing he remembers of those days, or just that it is the only thing he will tell me.

He is such a strong, handsome, caring man, a successful businessman, a loving father and husband. But I believe that subconsciously he has a great fear, a fear he doesn't understand. Often, I see panic in his eyes. It comes and goes quickly. And it happens anywhere, any time. It can happen today when we have lunch. He is able to control it. Yet sometimes I think that great discipline of his that controls that panic is somehow working against him. I don't know. There are no answers. There is only that he was lost, and I found him, and the person I found was both different from and the same as the person I lost. But, ultimately, my finding him is all that really matters.

War doesn't end with the signing of a piece of paper. War goes on forever in the lives of those who experienced it, in our thoughts and feelings, and in those places of the spirit too deep for thoughts and feelings. Alex and I will continue, however inadequately, to search for each other. Will we ever find each other? I don't know. When your love is a searching, and your searching is love, then survival, for both Alex and me, must always be a way of life.

"It's a beautiful day. Let's walk to the Franklin Café. Would you like that?"

"Yes Alex, I'd like that. I'd like that very much."

BRIGITTE BARRELL was born in Dresden, Germany. She attended private and finishing schools and studied at the University of Munich. After the bombing of Dresden she fled to the Bavarian Alps, where she spent several years. In 1952 she immigrated to the United States with her two sons. She opened a regional office for Manpower, Inc. temporary help services in 1953. In 1972 she became Honorary Consul of the Federal Republic of Germany. She has recently retired from Manpower, Inc. but is retained as a consultant for the company and continues to perform her duties as Consul.

Mrs. Barrell lives in New York State with her husband, Nathaniel, who is an attorney. They have three children. Their daughter, Brigitte ("Gitti"), is currently writing a screen adaption of her mother's book.

BRENT FILSON has published fifteen books on a variety of subjects and currently lives in Massachusetts with his wife and children.

D 811.5 .B24 1992

Barrell, Brigitte.

Another bridge